PRAISE FOR ARE THESE THE LAST DAYS?

Greg Laurie writes like he preaches. He makes the Bible come to life. This book on the timely subject of the last days is true to the prophetic Scripture and should be read by everyone as we approach the end of the age. I heartily endorse this book!

Tim LaHaye
Author, Minister and Educator

The tone of our times mandates that we ask ourselves if these are the last days and summons all believers to assess their heart toward Christ as He asks the question, "Are you serious about being ready and passionately living in anticipation of the blessed hope of My return?"

Jack W. Hayford
President, International Foursquare Church
Chancellor, The King's College and Seminary
Los Angeles, California

One of the biggest pitfalls that Christians can fall into is shortsightedness—living our lives for what is temporal without any thought of what lies ahead. In this inspiring work, Greg Laurie reminds us to look ahead at what is coming and to what matters most. I believe the words in this book will be a wonderful tool for evangelism. Yet once again Greg Laurie will be leading many to Christ!

Tommy Walker
Songwriter and Worship Leader
Author, *Songs from Heaven*

GREG LAURIE

ARE THESE THE
LAST DAYS?

Regal

From Gospel Light
Ventura, California, U.S.A.

PUBLISHED BY REGAL BOOKS
FROM GOSPEL LIGHT
VENTURA, CALIFORNIA, U.S.A.
PRINTED IN THE U.S.A.

Regal Books is a ministry of Gospel Light, a Christian publisher dedicated to serving the local church. We believe God's vision for Gospel Light is to provide church leaders with biblical, user-friendly materials that will help them evangelize, disciple and minister to children, youth and families.

It is our prayer that this Regal book will help you discover biblical truth for your own life and help you meet the needs of others. May God richly bless you.

For a free catalog of resources from Regal Books/Gospel Light, please call your Christian supplier or contact us at 1-800-4-GOSPEL *or* www.regalbooks.com.

Library of Congress Cataloging-in-Publication Data
Laurie, Greg.
Are these the last days? / Greg Laurie.
      p. cm.
Includes bibliographical references (p.   ).
ISBN 0-8307-3831-2 (trade paper)
1. End of the world. I. Title.
BT877.L38 2006
236'.9—dc22   2005027726

1   2   3   4   5   6   7   8   9   10   /   10   09   08   07   06   05

Rights for publishing this book in other languages are contracted by Gospel Light Worldwide, the international nonprofit ministry of Gospel Light. Gospel Light Worldwide also provides publishing and technical assistance to international publishers dedicated to producing Sunday School and Vacation Bible School curricula and books in the languages of the world. For additional information, visit www.gospellightworldwide.org; write to Gospel Light Worldwide, P.O. Box 3875, Ventura, CA 93006; or send an e-mail to info@gospellightworldwide.org.

CONTENTS

*HE WHO TESTIFIES TO THESE THINGS SAYS,
"SURELY I AM COMING QUICKLY."
AMEN. EVEN SO, COME, LORD JESUS!*

REVELATION 22:20

PREFACE

Tsunamis. Earthquakes. Hurricanes. Terrorism. War in the Middle East. Even the skeptics are beginning to ask, "Are we living in the last days? Are these the 'signs of the times' that the Bible tells us will happen before the return of Christ?"

When the Pharisees and Sadducees asked Jesus to show them a sign from heaven, He said, "'You know the saying, 'Red sky at night means fair weather tomorrow, red sky in the morning means foul weather all day.' You are good at reading the weather signs in the sky, but you can't read the obvious signs of the times!" (Matt. 16:2-3, *NLT*).

I believe that the events happening in our world right now are indeed the signs of the times. Jesus said, "Now when these things begin to happen, look up and lift up your heads, because your redemption draws near" (Luke 21:28). We are living in a time in which we are literally seeing Bible prophecy fulfilled before our very eyes.

In fact, there is at least one group of people today that officially tracks the signs of the times: a team of atomic scientists who oversee what is called the Doomsday Clock. This clock is either moved forward or back, depending on how imminent a nuclear war is believed to be. The clock has been moved only 17 times in 56 years, and it was most recently moved forward on February 27, 2002, due to "many disturbing developments in the world involving nuclear weapons."[1] The Doomsday Clock now reads seven minutes until midnight, or doomsday.

Is the end of the world near? Are we headed toward Armageddon? I would encourage you to prayerfully draw your own conclusions as you consider what is presented in the pages ahead.

In Luke 17, Jesus, speaking of His return, said:

When the Son of Man returns, the world will be like the people were in Noah's day. In those days before the flood, the people enjoyed banquets and parties and weddings right up to the time Noah entered his boat and the flood came to destroy them all. And the world will be as it was in the days of Lot. People went about their daily business—eating and drinking, buying and selling, farming and building—until the morning Lot left Sodom. Then fire and burning sulfur rained down from heaven and destroyed them all. Yes, it will be "business as usual" right up to the hour when the Son of Man returns (vv. 26-30, *NLT*).

Doesn't this sound a lot like today? As I look at the times in which we are living, they look strikingly similar to what this and other passages of Scripture are describing as Earth's final days. Are we living in them? I think we are. Will the Lord return in our lifetime? I don't know for sure, but I certainly hope He will. Whether He comes in my lifetime or not, I believe that His return is soon. Consider this: There has never been a generation that has been closer to the return of Christ than we are right now.

It reminds me of the story about a little boy who would frequently go to his grandmother's house for lunch. One of the things he especially enjoyed at her house was watching the old grandfather clock strike 12:00 P.M. It was one of those clocks that would chime every hour on the hour, and the number of chimes would correspond to the time of day. The little boy loved this clock. But on this particular day, something had gone wrong with the clock's inner mechanism. When the clock struck 12, instead of chiming 12 times, it chimed 13... 14... 15... and then 16 times. The boy ran excitedly into the kitchen where his grandmother was making lunch and exclaimed, "Grandma! Grandma! It's later than it's ever been before!"

That is an apt description of the times in which we are living right now. It is later than it's ever been before.

Comedian Jay Leno offered this humorous insight into the current state of our world during one of his opening monologues on *The Tonight Show*: "Hurricane Rita, this is like the ninth hurricane out this season. Maybe this isn't the time to take God out of the Pledge of Allegiance."[2]

Jay has a good point. Let's talk about it together.

Notes

1. "What Makes the Clock Tick?" *Bulletin of the Atomic Scientists*, March 25, 2003. http://www.thebulletin.org/issues/2003/wo/0325schwartz.html (accessed July 25, 2004).

2. Jay Leno, quoted on "Late Night Political Jokes," September 18-24, 2005. http://politicalhumor.about.com/library/bldailyfeed3.htm (accessed November 2, 2005).

ARE WE THERE YET?

*AND DO THIS, KNOWING THE TIME, THAT NOW IT IS
HIGH TIME TO AWAKE OUT OF SLEEP; FOR NOW OUR SALVATION
IS NEARER THAN WHEN WE FIRST BELIEVED.*

ROMANS 13:11

There are many religious books that people look to for guidance today. But there is only one book that dares to predict the future not once, not twice, but hundreds of times—and that book is the Bible.

In fact, a substantial portion of Holy Scripture is prophecy. Many of the Bible's prophecies have been fulfilled so far. Therefore, if many of the Bible's prophecies have already happened exactly as God said they would, I have no reason to doubt that the remaining ones will be fulfilled just as God's Word has predicted they will.

I remember hearing Pastor Chuck Smith of Calvary Chapel tell the story of how, in early November, he noticed Christmas decorations already up at the mall. He commented to his wife, Kay, "Honey, it is almost Thanksgiving."

She said, "These decorations are not up for Thanksgiving. They are up for Christmas."

He said, "I know, but if Christmas is close, Thanksgiving is closer."

That is a good analogy for the times in which we are living. When we see the signs of the times around us, showing, for instance, that the Antichrist could emerge at any time, we know the return of Jesus Christ is even closer.

Let's consider another analogy: labor pains. We find a key statement in Mark 13:8 at the conclusion of a list of events that

CHAPTER 1

will take place in the last days: "These are the beginnings of sorrows." Here, the word "sorrows" could be translated "birth pains." The apostle Paul, describing the time leading up to the coming of the Lord, said:

> For you know quite well that the day of the Lord will come unexpectedly, like a thief in the night. When people are saying, 'All is well; everything is peaceful and secure,' then disaster will fall upon them as suddenly as a woman's birth pains begin when her child is about to be born. And there will be no escape (1 Thess. 5:2-3, *NLT*).

Any woman who has given birth knows that labor pains build up gradually and lead to the arrival of her child. That is how the Bible describes events of the last days. It will be like labor pains. You will see something take place that reminds you the Lord is coming back. Then maybe a little time will pass and you will see something else. Then you will start seeing a few things happen in rapid succession. What does that mean? It means that it is getting close to the Lord's return.

We are seeing things happen on a yearly basis—and even on a monthly basis—that remind us Jesus Christ is coming back.

I believe we are living in that time right now. We are seeing things happen on a yearly basis—and even on a monthly basis—that remind us Jesus Christ is coming back.

A LOOK AT THE PROPHETIC CALENDAR

What are the signs, or birth pains, so to speak, that we should be looking for? Jesus' disciples asked Him this very question: "Now as He sat on the Mount of Olives, the disciples came to

Him privately, saying, 'Tell us, when will these things be? And what will be the sign of Your coming, and of the end of the age?'" (Matt. 24:3).

Before we look at the Lord's answer, let's take a moment to revisit the events that led up to this important question. It all began with the disciples' admiration of the temple: "As Jesus was leaving the Temple grounds, his disciples pointed out to him the various Temple buildings" (Matt. 24:1, *NLT*). Mark's Gospel gives us even greater detail. One of the disciples exclaimed, "Teacher, look at these tremendous buildings! Look at the massive stones in the walls!" (Mark 13:1, *NLT*).

There was no exaggerating here. The Jewish Temple was considered one of the great wonders of the ancient world. Under construction for 46 years at this point, it was near completion, which would come in A.D. 63, a mere 7 years before it was destroyed. Located in a place where it had dominance over ancient Jerusalem, historians described the Temple as appearing like a mountain of gold because of its nine massive gates. The incredible size of the foundation stones was the equivalent of a railroad boxcar. The Temple was a magnificent structure. It would be startling to look at even today, much less at that particular time in history.

Jesus said, "Do you see all these buildings? I assure you, they will be so completely demolished that not one stone will be left on top of another!" (Matt. 24:2, *NLT*). The disciples' jaws must have dropped when Jesus made that statement. They probably thought, "Are you kidding? There is no way you could dismantle the Temple, even if you wanted to." It would have been just as far-fetched if someone had said on September 10, 2001, "I predict that the Twin Towers of the World Trade Center will come crashing to the ground in one day." Who would have thought that such a thing was possible? But they did fall. In a similar way, it wouldn't have seemed possible to the disciples that the Temple could be dismantled.

Jesus was describing something that was in their future but that is now in our past. With 20/20 hindsight, we can look back at what Jesus was pointing toward and see that these events happened exactly as our Lord said they would. In A.D. 70, the Roman general, Titus, built large, wooden scaffolds around the walls of the Temple buildings, piled them high with wood and other flammable items, and set them ablaze. The fires were so intense that the stones of the Temple crumpled. To retrieve the melted gold from the temple walls, Roman troops dismantled the Temple stone by stone, fulfilling exactly the prediction of Jesus Christ. Why is that important? Because if this happened as Jesus said it would, and other things happened as Jesus said they would, then we know that what is yet to come also will happen just as He said.

SIGNS OF THE TIMES

This brings us back to the disciples' question. Remember, they approached Jesus privately and asked Him what would be the signs of His return and of the end of the world. Here is what Jesus told them:

> Take heed that no one deceives you. For many will come in My name, saying, "I am the Christ," and will deceive many. And you will hear of wars and rumors of wars. See that you are not troubled; for all these things must come to pass, but the end is not yet. For nation will rise against nation, and kingdom against kingdom. And there will be famines, pestilences, and earthquakes in various places. All these are the beginning of sorrows (Matt. 24:4-8).

In the verses above, Jesus gives a number of last-days signs that we should be looking for.

An Explosion of Religious Deception

In the last days, there will be an emergence of false teachers, false prophets, gurus, and so forth who will claim that they are the Messiah (see Matt. 24:4-5). This will culminate in the emergence of the ultimate deceiver, the Antichrist.

For many years now, we have witnessed an explosion of cults, such as Jehovah's Witnesses, the Mormons (also known as The Church of Jesus Christ of Latter-day Saints), the Christian Science Church, the Church of Scientology, and other groups. Then there have been newer cults like the followers of Jim Jones who committed mass suicide in Guyana in 1978; the Branch Davidians and their leader, David Koresh, who died in a stand-off with federal agents in Texas in 1993; and the Heaven's Gate suicides in Southern California in 1997.

There also has been an explosion of New Age mysticism and spirituality in recent years. I find it interesting how many people today will say, "I am spiritual, but I am not into organized religion." It is their way of saying that they want to have a belief system, but they want to live as they choose. So many people today talk about how they have found their own truth and their own path. I believe all of this is pointing to the emergence of the Antichrist and the beginning of the Tribulation period described in Revelation 6:

> Now I saw when the Lamb opened one of the seals; and I heard one of the four living creatures saying with a voice like thunder, "Come and see." And I looked, and behold, a white horse. He who sat on it had a bow; and a crown was given to him, and he went out conquering and to conquer (vv. 1-2).

Who is this rider these verses are speaking of? Is it Jesus Christ? No, it is the Antichrist. I find it interesting that he rides a white horse and has a crown, because we read later on in Revelation that when Christ comes back, He will be riding a white horse and will be wearing many crowns (see Rev. 19:11-12). This reminds us that the Antichrist is essentially an imitator. He is an imitation of the real thing.

The prefix "anti-" not only means "against" but also means "instead of." In many ways, the Antichrist, or the Beast as he is also called, masquerades as the Messiah. The Antichrist will succeed where others have failed. He will bring temporary solutions politically, militarily and economically. In fact, his accomplishments will be so spectacular, far-reaching and unprecedented that many will hail him as the very Messiah. But in time he will impose his own religion on the world and will have his false prophet working alongside him. (We will discuss this further in chapter 4.)

Wars and Rumors of Wars

This leads us to another sign pointing toward the last days, which will be "wars and rumors of wars" (see Matt. 24:6). Think of all the wars our planet has seen so far in its history. We know that more than 10 million people lost their lives in World War I, which was thought of as the war that would end all wars. But it took only 20 years for a new and even more terrible war to develop. During World War II, 50 million people died.

These wars, as horrible as they were, will not compare to the scale of war that will be unleashed by Satan during the Tribulation period. How it will happen, we don't know. It could be cataclysmic. We know that God could pour out His wrath on the earth. Then again, God could allow humanity to unleash all the weaponry that it has been amassing for years now.

To date, nations with nuclear weapons have been able to keep one another at bay. But now there are rogue nations that have gotten hold of nuclear weapons. Some terrorist organizations have been trying to obtain them for some time. It could be that, in this terrible war, all of that nuclear weaponry would be released. As the late President Ronald Reagan said, "Man has used every weapon he has ever devised. It takes no crystal ball to perceive that a nuclear war is likely, and in nuclear war, all mankind would lose."[1] Such war would give an explanation as to the global famine and pestilence that will follow the emergence of the Antichrist.

Famines and Pestilences

In addition to "wars and rumors of wars," global famine and pestilence will be one of the signs of the last days (see Rev. 6:8). Contrary to what some may think, famine isn't a problem of the past. According to the United Nations' World Food Program, more than 800 million people go hungry every day, while 24 thousand people die each day from hunger and hunger-related causes.[2]

When it comes to global pestilences, think of what has happened in our generation alone. Thirty-eight million people presently live with HIV-AIDS. Of these, 95 percent live in developing nations, mostly on the African continent, where there is a pandemic of AIDS.[3] Eight thousand people die every day of the AIDS virus.[4] Certainly this would be one of the things the Bible is speaking of. Also, it seems that on a regular basis, some new kind of epidemic is breaking out, more recent ones being SARS and the Bird Flu.

As we look at this and what is happening in our world, we can certainly see the birth pains that seem to be getting closer together.

Earthquakes, Hurricanes and Tsunamis

Jesus said, "And there will be great earthquakes in various places, and famines and pestilences; and there will be fearful sights and great signs from heaven" (Luke 21:11).

Consider the tsunami that struck Southeast Asia, December 26, 2004. It was caused by the fourth most powerful undersea earthquake on record—an earthquake so powerful that it moved the entire island of Sumatra 100 feet southwest of its original position. Geologists said the tsunami was so powerful that it set the whole earth vibrating. It interfered with the earth's rotation to the degree that time stopped for three microseconds.

According to the U.S. Geological Society, the occurrence of earthquakes is on the rise. For the past 50 years, the number of recorded earthquakes has increased every decade—not just the minor ones, but the "killer" quakes as well. The earthquake that caused the tsunami that struck Southeast Asia was one of the strongest ever, with more than 286,000 casualties in its wake. More earthquakes will come.

Then there is the devastation of Hurricane Katrina. All of these are signs of the times.

Religious Persecution

Another sign of the times will be persecution. Jesus said, "But watch out for yourselves, for they will deliver you up to councils, and you will be beaten in the synagogues. And you will be brought before rulers and kings for My sake, for a testimony to them. And the gospel must first be preached to all the nations" (Mark 13:9-10).

We have seen persecution against the Church for centuries. There was a martyr period in Church history that extended from A.D. 100 to A.D. 314, where literally thousands and thousands of courageous men, women and children stood up for their faith with their blood. Many secular historians suggest there were 10 great persecutions intended to wipe out Christianity, beginning with Caesar Nero and ending with the Roman emperor, Diocletian.

During this time, believers were fed alive to wild animals. They were killed in Roman arenas for sport. They were torn apart, tortured, burned at the stake and crucified. Diocletian felt that he had been so successful in eradicating Christianity from the face of the earth that he had a coin struck that read, "The Christian religion is destroyed and the worship of the Roman gods are restored." Needless to say, Diocletian was proved wrong. Instead of being destroyed by persecution, the Church actually grew stronger.

We need to remember that if we are true followers of Jesus, we too will be persecuted. The Bible says, "All who desire to live godly in Christ Jesus will suffer persecution" (2 Tim. 3:12). In John 15, Jesus said:

> If the world hates you, you know that it hated Me before it hated you. If you were of the world, the world would love its own. Yet because you are not of the world, but I chose you out of the world, therefore the world hates you. Remember the word that I said to you, "A servant is not greater than his master." If they persecuted Me, they will also persecute you (vv. 18-20).

When we as believers stand up for our faith, it will make some people angry, especially when we declare that Jesus Christ is the only way to God (see John 14:6). In our pluralistic society of moral relativism, when someone makes a statement such as, "All roads don't lead to God—only one road leads to God; all truth is not yours to choose—there is only one real truth, and Jesus Christ is the only way to God," some people will not like it.

In fact, in our own country today, we see our religious liberties evaporating before our eyes. For example, in 1962, the U.S. Supreme Court found prayer in public schools unconstitutional. In 1980, the Court banned the posting of the Ten Commandments in public schools. In 1989, the Court ruled that a nativity scene in a government building was unconstitutional. In 1992, prayer by clergy members at public school graduation ceremonies was ruled unconstitutional. In 2003, Alabama Chief Justice Roy Moore was removed from office for refusing to remove a Ten Commandments monument from the state's Supreme Court building. And at the time of this writing, a national debate is underway as to whether marriage should be defined as a union between one man and one woman and whether or not we

Persecution will only get worse in the last days—that is what Scripture tells us.

should keep the phrase "One Nation Under God" in the Pledge of Allegiance.

To quote Jay Leno again, "So what does happen if you get arrested for saying the words 'under God' while reciting the pledge? You go before a judge and have to take an oath to 'swear to tell the truth, the whole truth and nothing but the truth so help me GOD.'"[5] Things we never thought possible have become realities.

Here in the United States, some people have been attacked physically—even killed—because of their faith in Christ. Fresh in our memories are the tragic shootings at Columbine High School in 1999, where 13 people lost their lives. Among them were Cassie Bernall and Rachel Scott, who were singled out for their Christian faith.

Outside U.S. borders, we know that persecution is far worse. For example, thousands of Christians in Sudan have been beaten, driven from their homes, and martyred for their faith. In Iraq, the radical Muslim group responsible for the kidnapping and murder of Kim Sun-il of South Korea in June 2004 claimed they killed him because he "tried to propagate Christianity in Iraq."[6]

Persecution will only get worse in the last days—that is what Scripture tells us.

Jerusalem as an International Focal Point

Jerusalem, the city of David, has always had a central role in Scripture, and it figures prominently in prophecies about the last days in which God will "restore the fortunes" of Jerusalem (see Jer. 32:44; Dan. 9:25; Joel 3:1). In Mark 13:28-29, Jesus said the rebirth of Israel will be a supersign of the last days: "Now learn this parable from the fig tree: When its branch has already become tender, and puts forth leaves, you know that summer is near. So you also, when you see these things happening, know that it is near—at the doors!"

On more than one occasion in Scripture, Israel is compared to a fig tree (see Judg. 9:11; Hos. 9:10; Joel 1:7-8). I believe that Mark 13:28-29, along with many other Scripture passages, such as Ezekiel 37-39, speak of the rebirth of Israel—the regathering of God's people. When the nation of Israel comes back into existence, Jesus was stating prophetically, it is a supersign that His coming is near.

Of course, we know that this prophecy was fulfilled not that long ago. On May 14, 1948, David Ben-Gurion stood before the masses gathered in Tel Aviv and declared Israel's independence. Israel announced to the world that she was once again to be a free state. Having lost six million Jews to Nazi concentration camps, the Jewish people began returning to the very land that God had given to them centuries before. It was unprecedented in human history for a nation to essentially cease to exist and then to come back into existence.

After the state of Israel was declared in 1948, five Arab states came against Israel and the resulting war left the city of Jerusalem divided. Jordan retained control over the old city, including the Temple mount and most historic sites. During the six-day war in 1967, Israeli forces once again captured the old city and reunified all of Jerusalem. The city of Jerusalem was under Jewish control for the first time in many centuries. Bible prophecy had been fulfilled perfectly.

God said, "I will make Jerusalem and Judah like an intoxicating drink to all the nearby nations that send their armies to besiege Jerusalem. On that day I will make Jerusalem a heavy stone, a burden for the world. None of the nations who try to lift it will escape unscathed" (Zech. 12:2-3, *NLT*). So when God says that Jerusalem will be the focal point of the last-days scenario, we see this already happening.

You can hardly scan today's headlines without reading about conflict in the Middle East. So often it centers on Jerusalem. There are many, many passages of Scripture that specifically say Jerusalem will be at the heart of it all. Jerusalem, of course, remains at the heart of the Israeli-Palestinian conflict. Many Arab leaders worldwide insist that the old city and entire West Bank are rightfully Palestinian territory and must be ceded back as a condition for peace. Scripture tells us that God will gather all the nations of the world together against Jerusalem (see Zech. 12:2-3; 14:2). The only true peace that will ever come is when the King of kings, Lord of lords, and the Prince of Peace comes back and establishes His kingdom on Earth. This is what we need to be looking for.

WHERE DO WE GO FROM HERE?

So what is all this about? Are we really in the last days? The answer is yes. What we see today are the labor pains of what is yet to come. As we watch these things happen in our world, as we sense these labor pains getting closer and closer together, they tell us the coming of Jesus Christ is near. In fact, I see nothing in Scripture that needs to occur before the Rapture of the Church can take place. In my understanding of Bible prophecy, it is the next event on the prophetic calendar. And it could happen at any time.

Notes

1. Billy Graham, *Till Armageddon: A Perspective on Suffering* (Waco, TX: Word Publishing, 1984), n.p.
2. Office of International Information Programs, U.S. Department of State, Address by United Nations Secretary-General Kofi Annan to the World Food Summit, Rome, June 10, 2002. http://usinfo.org/wf-archive/2002/020610/epf110.htm (accessed September 2005).
3. U.S. Department of State, International Information Programs, "World Food Program to Cosponsor U.N. HIV/AIDS Program," October 16, 2003.http://usinfo.state.gov/xarchives/display.html?p=washfile-english&y=2003&m=October&x=20031016143623retropc0.9115106&t=xarchives/xarchitem.html (accessed September 2005).
4. Testimony from Medecins Sans Frontieres for the Senate Foreign Relations Committee Subcommittee on African Affairs Hearing on "Fighting HIV/AIDS in Africa: A Progress Report," delivered by Lulu Oguda, M.D., April 7, 2004. http://www.doctorswithoutborders.org/publications/speeches/2004/hiv_testimony_04-07-2004.cfm (accessed September 2005).
5. Jay Leno, quoted at "The Pledge of Allegiance" blog, frappydoo.com. http://frappydoo.com/forum/showpost.php?p=53513&postcount=5 (accessed November 2, 2005).
6. Reuben Staines, "Church Leaders Condemn 'Religious Killing' of Kim Sun-il," *The Korea Times*, July 15, 2004. http://times.hankooki.com/.

THE NEXT EVENT ON THE PROPHETIC CALENDAR

*SO ALSO CHRIST DIED ONLY ONCE AS A SACRIFICE TO TAKE AWAY
THE SINS OF MANY PEOPLE. HE WILL COME AGAIN BUT NOT TO DEAL
WITH OUR SINS AGAIN. THIS TIME HE WILL BRING SALVATION
TO ALL THOSE WHO ARE EAGERLY WAITING FOR HIM.*

HEBREWS 9:28, NLT

It seems to me that the next even on the prophetic calendar is the rapture of the Church. If you have been looking for the word "rapture" in the Bible, you won't find it. Unless you have a Latin translation, that is. The phrase "caught up" is the Latin word *rapturus*, which means "to be caught up." A more literal definition is "to be snatched up." Believers will be taken to meet the Lord in the air.

The apostle Paul described this event in his letter to the Christians at Thessalonica:

> For the Lord Himself will descend from heaven with a shout, with the voice of an archangel, and with the trumpet of God. And the dead in Christ will rise first. Then we who are alive and remain shall be caught up together with them in the clouds to meet the Lord in the air. And thus we shall always be with the Lord (1 Thess. 4:16-17).

But Paul wasn't the only one to speak of the Rapture. Jesus mentioned it in Matthew 24, where He said, "Then two men will be in the field: one will be taken and the other left. Two women will be grinding at the mill: one will be taken and the other left. Watch therefore, for you do not know what hour your Lord is coming" (vv. 40-42). Jesus also spoke of it in John 14, where He said, "In My Father's house are many mansions; if it were not so, I would have told you. I go to prepare a place for you. And if I go and prepare a place for you, I will come again and receive you to Myself; that where I am, there you may be also" (vv. 2-3).

We also find a reference to the Rapture in 1 John 2:28 and 3:3, "Abide in Him, that when He appears, we may have confidence and not be ashamed before Him at His coming. Beloved, now we are children of God; and it has not yet been revealed what we shall be, but we know that when He is revealed, we shall be like Him, for we shall see Him as He is."

THE BIG PICTURE

Let's look at the big picture of end-time prophecy, which we will study more closely in the chapters ahead.

Home in an Instant

Returning for a moment to Paul's description of the Rapture in 1 Thessalonians 4, note that verse 17 says that Christians who are living at the time of the Rapture "shall be caught up together with them [the dead in Christ] in the clouds to meet the Lord in the air." The word "meet" in this verse carries the idea of meeting a royal person or a person of great importance. When the Lord calls us to Himself, we will meet the ultimate royalty, the King of kings and the Lord of lords.

> **When the Lord calls us to Himself, we will meet the ultimate royalty, the King of kings and the Lord of lords.**

We see from these verses about the Rapture that Christians will be received into the presence of God instantaneously. According to 1 Corinthians 15:51-52, "We shall not all sleep, but we shall all be changed—in a moment, in the twinkling of an eye, at the last trumpet. For the trumpet will sound, and the dead will be raised incorruptible, and we shall be changed." Note that this verse doesn't say "in the blink of an eye," but rather "in the twinkling of an eye." A blink is fast—so fast that most of the time you don't even notice it when you blink—but the time it takes for an eye to twinkle is even faster.

There might be some who think they will have time to decide whether to believe when the Rapture happens. But no one can decide that fast. Anyone who has waited until the last minute will be left behind, and they will have to go through the Tribulation. However, if you have put your faith in Jesus Christ, you have the hope that you will be taken before the Tribulation period comes. The Bible says, "For God did not appoint us to wrath, but to obtain salvation through our Lord Jesus Christ" (1 Thess. 5:9). In the flash of a second, every living Christian on Earth will suddenly and instantaneously be gone. So, you might go to bed one night and wake up in heaven.

One night, as my wife, Cathe, and I were lying in bed and talking, she said, "Isn't it wonderful that one day we will meet the Lord in the air? Wouldn't it be exciting if it happened in our lifetime? Can you imagine? We would be lying here in bed, maybe talking, maybe sleeping, and all of a sudden, we are right there in the presence of God?" As she described this, being the prankster that I am, I thought it would be funny to secretly slip out of bed. So I quietly crept down on the floor without her knowing. "Wouldn't it be great, Greg?" Cathe continued. "Greg?" She reached over to my side of the bed . . . but I wasn't there. "Greg!" she screamed. "Greg!" Meanwhile, I was lying on the floor, laughing. But the real Rapture will not be a laughing matter. It could happen at any moment, when we least expect it.

Don't Plan on It

This brings me to a frequently asked question about the Rapture: Can we predict the date? The answer is no, we cannot. What about the people who say they have somehow broken the code and have figured it out? Should we believe them? No, we should not. Under no circumstances should we believe anyone who tells us that they know the date of the Lord's return.

Why? Because Jesus said, "No one knows the day or the hour when these things will happen, not even the angels in heaven or the Son himself. Only the Father knows" (Matt. 24:36, *NLT*). Now, if you were to translate this verse from the original language, it would read, "No one knows the day or the hour." So what that actually means is, "No one knows the day or the hour." In other words, Jesus said what He meant and meant what He said. So don't buy into the nonsense that we can predict when the Rapture will occur. The Bible simply tells us to be ready for it.

While no one knows when the Rapture will take place, I can give you an educated guess as to when the Second Coming of Christ will take place. Of course, I can't give you a specific date, but I can tell you that the Second Coming will occur seven years after the Rapture takes place, following the Great Tribulation period.

The Rapture and the Second Coming

Sometimes people confuse the Rapture and the Second Coming. Here are some differences: The Rapture will occur *before* the Tribulation, while the Second Coming will occur *after* the Tribulation. At the Rapture, Jesus will come *before* the time of judgment. At the time of the Second Coming, Jesus will come *with* that judgment. The Rapture is *for* His people. The Second Coming is Jesus *with* His people.

The Bible teaches that when Christ returns in the Second Coming, He will be joined by saints arrayed in fine linen (see Rev. 19:14). It will be the ultimate Holy Land tour, directed by Jesus Christ Himself as He establishes His kingdom on Earth. In the Rapture, Jesus will come like a thief in the night (see Matt. 24:42-43; Luke 12:39-40). In the Second Coming, everyone will see Him (see Rev. 1:7). Jesus said, "For as the lightning comes from the east and flashes to the west, so also will the coming of the Son of Man be" (Matt. 24:27).

A Glimpse of the Future

Somewhere close in proximity to the time of the Rapture, many nations will join together and attack Israel. A large force from the extreme north of Israel, identified in the Bible as Magog (believed by many scholars to be modern-day Russia), will join with allies that are hostile toward Israel.

When Israel is attacked, the Bible says that God will intervene, defend Israel, and turn back the majority of that attacking army. The weapons from that war will be burned for seven years, and there will be a great revival. Many believe that this battle will occur right before the tribulation period, because a seven-year chronology follows. But sometime before, during, or right after this battle, it seems, the Rapture of the Church will take place.

A coming world leader will then arrive on the scene. The Bible calls him the Antichrist, the Beast. He will be a charismatic and powerful economic and military leader who will be able to do what no other leader has ever been able to do. He will develop a peace treaty between the Jews and the Arabs in which both sides *will actually* stop their fighting. The Antichrist will establish a treaty that will work, and he will even help the Jews rebuild their Temple.

After the Temple has been rebuilt, halfway into the seven-year Tribulation, the Antichrist will show his true colors. He will erect an image of himself in the Temple and command people to worship it. There also will be a mark that people will be required to take in order to buy or sell things.

The seven-year tribulation will culminate in the Battle of Armageddon. It will be the war to end all wars, fought in the Valley of Megiddo. Then, Jesus Christ will visibly return to the earth in the Second Coming and will establish His kingdom. We know this as the millennial reign of Christ.

THE RELEVANCE OF THE RAPTURE

As I mentioned, this is the big picture, which we will study more closely in the chapters ahead. Now let's consider what the Rapture means for Christians today who have put their faith in Christ.

The Rapture Means No Death

There is a generation that will not see death, a generation that will not have to go to the grave. This generation of people will be caught up into the presence of the Lord. Are we that generation? I don't know. We very well could be, but no one can say with complete certainty.

> **Whether or not the Lord comes in my lifetime, my hope is not in the coming of the Lord, but in the fact that the Lord is coming.**

Whether or not the Lord comes in my lifetime, my hope is not in the coming of the Lord, but in the fact that the Lord is coming. I know that I will go to heaven one day, either by the Rapture or by death. These are just two different forms of transportation, like taking a taxi or a bus. In all honesty, there is no question in my mind that the Rapture would be preferable, but at the same time, I know that I am going to go to heaven.

What is exciting to me is not *how* I get to that final destination, but *where* that destination is that I am going. If the Lord comes during my lifetime, that is great. If He doesn't, that is fine as well. God knows what He is doing. As 2 Peter 3:9 tells us, "The Lord isn't really being slow about his promise to return, as some people think. No, he is being patient for your sake. He does not want anyone to perish, so he is giving more time for everyone to repent" (*NLT*). One way or another, whether it's through death or through the Rapture, we all will stand before God one day. We need to be ready to meet the Lord.

The Rapture Means a Reunion

Not only will we meet the Lord in the Rapture, but also we will be reunited with our friends and loved ones who have died and gone to be with the Lord. Death is the great separator, but Jesus Christ is the great reconciler. One day, you could be thinking about a loved one who has gone on to be with the Lord, when all of a sudden, instantaneously, you are looking that person in the face. The Rapture could happen that quickly.

It would also appear from another passage of Scripture that we also will be reunited with those whom we helped lead to Christ. Paul said to the Thessalonians, to whom he had ministered, "For what is our hope, or joy, or crown of rejoicing? Is it not even you in the presence of our Lord Jesus Christ at His coming?" (1 Thess. 2:19). Paul was saying that his spiritual children would be his crown of rejoicing in the Lord's presence when He comes. From this, it would appear that when we are caught up to be with the Lord, each of us will have grouped around us those whom we helped to bring to Christ. What an amazing thought.

You may not realize all those whom you have helped to bring to Christ. You may have had an impact on someone that you never even knew about. You may have never talked to that person about your faith in Christ. He may have just watched you and, by carefully observing your life, gained a positive impression of Christianity. Then, maybe God brought another Christian who said a few words to that person, which caused his heart to get a little softer. The little seed that was planted by your example was watered. Maybe another Christian came along and shared the gospel. Then yet another Christian invited that individual to church, where he committed his life to Christ.

The fact is that all of those people were a part of the conversion process, from the one who first sowed the seed to the one who invited that person to church. We never know how God might be using us to touch the life of another person. We are not going to know all those upon whom we have made an impact until we are with the Lord. In the meantime, we need to make the most of every opportunity to reach people for Christ. Sow the seed when you can. Water the seed others have sown. If God gives you the opportunity, reap where others have sown and watered. One day, when you get to heaven, you will be able to look back and see the small part (or perhaps the large part) you played in this (see 1 Cor. 3:5-11). All the mockery, all the laughter, and all the rejection you experienced as you tried to share the gospel will be worth it when you realize that these people are in heaven, in part because you obeyed the Lord in this area.

THE CURE FOR TROUBLED HEARTS

In speaking of the Lord's return, the Bible tells us many times to be ready. We should be alert and be watching. But, let me add, we shouldn't be afraid.

September 11, 2001 is a day we should never forget. We have all been affected by what happened on the horrific morning in New York City, Washington D.C., and a place called Shanksville in the Pennsylvania countryside. Our nation will never be the same. Now there are more threats. The question on everyone's mind is, What will happen next? It is amazing to consider how we entered the twenty-first century with so much optimism. Remember all the great celebrations? Now there is a lot of fear.

In John 14, Jesus spoke to a group of people who were frightened, troubled and agitated by what was happening around them. Here is what He had to say:

> Let not your heart be troubled; you believe in God, believe also in Me. In My Father's house are many mansions; if it were not so, I would have told you. I go to prepare a place for you. And if I go and prepare a place for you, I will come again and receive you to Myself; that where I am, there you may be also (vv. 1-3).

The word "troubled," in verse 1 means "don't be agitated, disturbed or thrown into confusion." How could we not feel this way in light of all that is happening in the world? Jesus gives us three reasons in these verses.

1. We Can Take God at His Word

"You believe in God, believe also in Me" (John 14:1). In the original language, this is a command. Jesus was saying, "I am telling you . . . I am ordering you . . . you believe in God, also believe in Me. Believe that I know what I am doing and that I will return for you. Your agitation is a result of not believing what God has said. You don't have the big picture, but one day, it all will become clear to you." In other words, we will have to trust Him on this. We may not understand, but we must believe in Him. We must take Him at His word.

Things that happen in life can stress us out—not only what happens nationally and globally, but also personally. We have some kind of health problem. A tragedy hits, and it seems as though our world has come to an end. But we need to remember that God is still on the throne. He is still in control of our lives.

We remember that tragic day in September as 9/11, which of course is the number we dial in an emergency. But we also need to remember Psalm 91:1: "He who dwells in the secret place of the Most High shall abide under the shadow of the Almighty." This passage goes on to say, "I will say of the Lord, 'He is my refuge and my fortress; My God, in Him I will trust.' You shall not be afraid of the terror by night, nor of the arrow that flies by day, nor of the pestilence that walks in darkness, nor of the destruction that lays waste at noonday" (vv. 2,5-6).

As Christians, we do not have to be afraid, regardless of what is going on in the world. Mark that in your mind. My future as a Christian is as bright as the promises of God. No matter what happens, I know that God is still in control of my life. The same is true for you.

The Bible teaches that God appoints the day of our birth and also the hour of our death. Job 14:5 says, "You have decided the length of our lives. You know how many months we will live, and we are not given a minute longer" (*NLT*). God determines when each of us will die, not some terrorist organization or anyone else for that matter. Therefore, we don't need to live in irrational fear and panic and anxiety.

This is not to say that we should not be careful and take precautions. But it is to say that God decided when we would live, and He also decides when we will die (or are taken up in the Rapture). As Paul said, "For to me, to live is Christ, and to die is gain" (Phil. 1:21). If you are a Christian, it is a win-win situation. Although there is cause to be troubled, there is greater cause not to be. Regardless of what you are facing, take God at His word.

2. We Have the Hope of Heaven
If you have put your faith in Jesus Christ, you will go to heaven when you die. Jesus said, "In My Father's house are many man-

sions; if it were not so, I would have told you. I go to prepare a place for you" (John 14:2). When we read the word "mansion" in this verse, it does not refer to a palatial estate like those in Beverly Hills. It doesn't mean that if you live a godly life, you will have a gorgeous megahome waiting for you on the other side; that if you were semi-committed, you will have a nice tract home; or that if you only went to church occasionally, you will have a little place with a half-moon cut in the door. That is not what this verse is saying.

When Jesus spoke of "many mansions," He was not speaking of a home in terms of a building as much as He was speaking of a new body that God has prepared for you. This phrase could just as easily be translated, "In my Father's house are many dwelling places." God will give us brand-new, resurrection bodies (see also 1 Cor. 15:51). So if someone was in a wheelchair on Earth, he will not be in one in heaven. If someone did not have the use of her eyes or her arms on Earth, she will have the use of them in heaven.

The human body was not meant to last forever. In fact, the Bible compares it to a tent: "For we know that if our earthly house, this tent, is destroyed, we have a building from God, a house not made with hands, eternal in the heavens" (2 Cor. 5:1). We do all sorts of things to try to prolong our lives. But eventually, our bodies will wear out. Philippians 3 reminds us:

> For our citizenship is in heaven, from which we also eagerly wait for the Savior, the Lord Jesus Christ, who will transform our lowly body that it may be conformed to His glorious body, according to the working by which He is able even to subdue all things to Himself (vv. 20-21).

We are going to heaven, where God will give each of us a new, glorified body. What a great hope. That is one reason we don't have to be afraid.

3. We Know That Jesus Is Coming Again

Jesus said, "I go to prepare a place for you. And if I go and prepare a place for you, I will come again and receive you to Myself; that where I am, there you may be also" (John 14:2-3). Jesus is speaking of the Rapture here.

Notice that Jesus says that He will come again and *receive* us unto Himself. He doesn't say that He will *take* us. He won't take us if we don't want to go. Hebrews 9:28 says, "To those who eagerly wait for Him He will appear a second time, apart from sin, for salvation." Are you eagerly waiting for the return of Jesus Christ? That is the kind of person whom Jesus is coming back for.

Are you ready?

A PREPARED PLACE
FOR PREPARED
PEOPLE

I AM GOING TO PREPARE A PLACE FOR YOU. . . .
WHEN EVERYTHING IS READY, I WILL COME AND GET YOU,
SO THAT YOU WILL ALWAYS BE WITH ME WHERE I AM.

JOHN 14:2-3, NLT

During the invitation at one of our evangelistic events, that we call Harvest Crusades, in Santa Barbara a few years ago, a 90-year-old man walked forward at the urging of his grandchild. His wife had died a few years before. She was a Christian and had prayed for him throughout her life. On her deathbed, she pleaded with her husband to give his life to Jesus Christ so that he could know the love and peace she had experienced. But he turned her down. So there he was at a Harvest Crusade. The service was coming to a close, and as I gave the invitation for people to walk forward and make a commitment to Jesus Christ, his granddaughter said, "Grandpa, do you want to go forward?"

"No."

"Come on," she said.

"It is cold down there. I don't want to go down there."

"Grandpa," she said, "I think you will like what you find down there."

"What do you think I am going to find down there?"

"You are going to find love and peace and life," she replied. So Grandpa slowly made his journey to the front of the stage, and he prayed the prayer and asked Christ to come into his life.

Afterward, he said, "Now I know what my wife was talking about. Now I know that I am going to see her again." And that is true for all Christians. We will again see our loved ones who have died as believers.

Heaven is the great hope of the Christian. It is a prepared place for prepared people. As you are reading this today, I hope you have made the most important preparation of all—getting your life right with God. If you have not done that, I encourage you to turn to the section at the back of this book entitled "How to Be Ready." There you will discover how you can be sure that you will go to heaven someday.

HOME, SWEET HOME

When you go to a movie theatre, you often see previews of coming attractions. These previews are called "trailers" in the movie industry, and they give you an idea of what the upcoming movie is about. How many times have you decided to see that movie based on the trailer you viewed, only to find that the preview was better than the actual film?

In Revelation 4, we find what we might call a sneak preview of what heaven will be like. It is hard for us, with our finite minds, to grasp the infinite. But this is what we will attempt as we look at this vivid and amazing description of heaven. As we look at this biblical "trailer," this preview of things to come, I want you to realize that the real thing will be far better than the preview.

This is a description from the apostle John as he is catapulted into eternity, where he sees supernatural things that he tries to describe in human terms:

> Then as I looked, I saw a door standing open in heaven, and the same voice I had heard before spoke to me with

the sound of a mighty trumpet blast. The voice said, "Come up here, and I will show you what must happen after these things." And instantly I was in the Spirit, and I saw a throne in heaven and someone sitting on it! The one sitting on the throne was as brilliant as gemstones—jasper and carnelian. And the glow of an emerald circled his throne like a rainbow. Twenty-four thrones surrounded him, and twenty-four elders sat on them. They were all clothed in white and had gold crowns on their heads. And from the throne came flashes of lightning and the rumble of thunder. And in front of the throne were seven lampstands with burning flames. They are the seven spirits of God. In front of the throne was a shiny sea of glass, sparkling like crystal. In the center and around the throne were four living beings, each covered with eyes, front and back (Rev. 4:1-6, *NLT*).

When we read these verses, we have to understand the limitations of the earthly language. John is trying to describe something that is beyond comprehension. It is breathtaking.

Have you ever seen or heard something that you could not possibly describe? For example, Hawaii is a beautiful place. But can you imagine trying to describe the beauty of the Hawaiian Islands to a three-month-old baby? It simply would be beyond that infant's comprehension. In the same way, we as human beings will not be able to fully grasp here in this life how glorious heaven will be. We will have to simply take God's word for it.

The apostle Paul had the privilege of actually going to heaven but then had to come back to Earth. Scripture tells us that as he was preaching in a certain place, He was stoned and thought to be dead (see Acts 14:19). I believe it was probably at this point that Paul was caught up into the presence of God and saw things beyond his human comprehension. But the Lord brought him back. I have often tried to envision that scene. Can you imagine? You are preaching the gospel. Then you are run out of town and stoned. Suddenly, you find yourself hurtled into the very presence of God.

"Lord, it is so good to be here! I am so thankful I am with You!" Paul might have said as he stood face-to-face with Jesus.

Perhaps the Lord responded, "Paul, I have some good news and some bad news. First, the good news. You will be coming back here."

"Coming back? Am I going somewhere?"

"That brings me to the bad news, Paul. There is a group of believers praying right now around your broken body, and I am sending you back because I have work for you to do."

"Lord, don't listen to them," Paul might have said. "They are sinners. Don't answer their prayers!"

Meanwhile back on Earth, the believers are fervently praying, "Lord, Paul is dead. What are we going to do? Bring our beloved friend and apostle back to us!" The color begins coming back to Paul's face. His hand starts moving. It is forming a fist. *Boom!* (At least that is what I would have done.)

Of course, Paul did no such thing. But he did come back to life, and then he went right back to the work that God had called him to. But here is what the resurrected apostle said about his brief stopover in heaven: "I was caught up into the third heaven fourteen years ago. Whether my body was there or just my spirit, I don't know; only God knows. But I do know that I was caught up into paradise and heard things so astounding that they cannot be told" (2 Cor. 12:2-4, *NLT*).

I love how candid Paul was about all of this. He could have boasted of all he saw, but instead he simply said it was beyond comprehension and description. He simply said that it was paradise!

I heard the story of a little girl and her dad who were looking up at the star-filled sky on a beautiful night. She said, "Daddy,

I have been thinking. If the wrong side of heaven is so beautiful, what will the right side be?" We are just seeing a glimpse of heaven. Think about how wonderful it will be.

WHAT WILL HEAVEN REALLY BE LIKE?

To begin with, there will be no night in heaven. Revelation 22:5 says, "And there will be no night there—no need for lamps or sun—for the Lord God will shine on them" (*NLT*). I remember visiting Franklin Graham in Alaska a number of years ago. We went out fishing one night for salmon. It was midnight, and yet there was still light. The good side about Alaska is that you have long days. The bad side is that you can have really long nights too.

> **In heaven, we will be able to walk the streets of gold with no concern for danger, because everything that causes fear will be eliminated.**

That is a little bit like how heaven will be. There will be no darkness, and there will be no more fear. You won't have to lock your doors. You won't need alarm systems. In heaven, we will be able to walk the streets of gold with no concern for danger, because everything that causes fear will be eliminated. What a comfort that is in these terror-filled times we are living in. In heaven, there will be no more suffering or death. Revelation 21 says:

> "Look, the home of God is now among his people! He will live with them, and they will be his people. God himself will be with them. He will remove all of their sorrows, and there will be no more death or sorrow or crying or pain. For the old world and its evils are gone forever."
>
> And the one sitting on the throne said, "Look, I am making all things new!" (vv. 3-5).

Sometimes I am asked whether we will remember people in heaven whom we once knew on Earth. I don't know for certain. It seems unlikely, however, that we would know less when we get there than we know now. But I do know this: In heaven, every one of your questions will be answered.

You may have some questions that you want to ask God. Maybe there was a tragedy that happened in your life and you don't understand it. Perhaps there is some issue that you have always grappled with. It could be that you have wondered about some circumstance in your life and thought, *Why has God allowed this?* Again, know this: Every question of yours will be answered in heaven. The Bible tells us, "Now we see things imperfectly as in a poor mirror, but then we will see everything with perfect clarity" (1 Cor. 13:12, *NLT*).

Actually, I think that when you get to heaven, stand before God Almighty and look into His eyes, you won't be pulling out your list of questions. I believe you will be falling down on your knees and worshiping Him, for all of your questions will be answered.

One of the questions often asked about heaven is whether we will see our loved ones again. Paul dealt with this topic when he wrote to the believers in Thessalonica. In chapter 2, we looked at 1 Thessalonians 4:16-17, in which Paul talks about the Rapture. But in the following verses, we also find Paul's response to the believers' question about departed loved ones who were believers:

> And now, brothers and sisters, I want you to know what will happen to the Christians who have died so you will not be full of sorrow like people who have no hope. For since we believe that Jesus died and was raised to life again, we also believe that when Jesus comes, God will bring back with Jesus all the Christians who have died.

Then, together with them, we who are still alive and
remain on the earth will be caught up in the clouds to
meet the Lord in the air and remain with him forever
(1 Thess. 4:13-14,17, *NLT*)

Will we see our loved ones who were believers again? According to these verses, absolutely.

I also believe that we will recognize one another in heaven.
Let me tell you why. Remember the story of Jesus on the Mount
of Transfiguration? Jesus had taken Peter, James and John up to
a high mountain, where He was transfigured before them, which
means He was shining like the sun. On each side of Him were
Moses and Elijah, and they were talking with Jesus.

Peter was so moved that he excitedly blurted out, "Lord, it is
good for us to be here; if You wish, let us make here three taber-
nacles: one for You, one for Moses, and one for Elijah" (Matt.
17:4). It is interesting that Peter recognized Moses and Elijah,
who had gone on to glory but had been brought back for a special "guest appearance" with Jesus. This means there was something about them that caused them to be recognizable to Peter.
Therefore, it would appear from this verse and others that in our
new bodies in heaven, there will be similarities to our old bodies,
yet at the same time, we will be in a glorified state.

Paul spoke of our recognizable bodies in heaven when he
said there are certain things that will be the same and certain
things that will be different.

But someone may ask, "How will the dead be raised?
What kind of bodies will they have?" What a foolish
question! When you put a seed into the ground, it
doesn't grow into a plant unless it dies first. And what
you put in the ground is not the plant that will grow, but
only a dry little seed of wheat or whatever it is you are

planting. It is the same way for the resurrection of the dead. Our earthly bodies, which die and decay, will be different when they are resurrected, for they will never die. Our bodies now disappoint us, but when they are raised, they will be full of glory. They are weak now, but when they are raised, they will be full of power (1 Cor. 15:35-37,42-43, *NLT*).

So if you are looking for a loved one in heaven, remember, there will be similarities, but there will be differences too, because we will be in our new bodies. But the most glorious thing of all about heaven—even better than the absence of darkness and sorrow and pain and death, and even better than being reunited with loved ones—is the fact that Jesus will be there. We will be with Christ, never to be separated from Him again.

THE ULTIMATE AWARDS CEREMONY

The Bible speaks of a coming day when rewards will be given out in heaven. Jesus spoke of this in Luke 14:14 when He said, "Then at the resurrection of the godly, God will reward you for inviting those who could not repay you" (*NLT*). Also in Revelation 22:12, Jesus said, "And behold, I am coming quickly, and My reward is with Me, to give to every one according to his work." This significant event that will take place in heaven, for which we should be preparing ourselves, is called the Judgment Seat of Christ.

In 2 Corinthians 5, we find a description of this Judgment Seat of Christ, before which every believer will stand:

Therefore we make it our aim, whether present or absent, to be well pleasing to Him. For we must all appear before the judgment seat of Christ, that each one may receive the things done in the body, according to what he has done, whether good or bad (vv. 9-10).

This is a very important statement: "We must all appear before the judgment seat of Christ." Understand that there is a difference between the Great White Throne Judgment described in Revelation 20:11-15 and the Judgment Seat of Christ. The Great White Throne Judgment is the final judgment for unbelievers. Revelation 20:15 says, "And anyone not found written in the Book of Life was cast into the lake of fire." If you are a Christian, you won't be there, and neither will I. But if you are an unbeliever, you will stand at that Great White Throne Judgment, and then it will be too late.

So we see that the Judgment Seat of Christ does not determine whether you will go to heaven. The Judgment Seat of Christ takes place in heaven, as a Christian, you already will be there. This judgment is about rewards. Second Corinthians 5:9-10 tell us, "Everything will be made clear and open, according to what we have done, whether it be good or bad." The word used here for "bad" doesn't speak of something that is necessarily ethically or morally evil. The immoral and sinful things that we have done have been forgiven, because of the death of Jesus on the cross. The word here for "bad" means "good for nothingness." It speaks of wasting our lives and the time, talent and resources God has given us. All of these things are to be used for His glory.

We were placed on the earth not to chase after personal fulfillment but to glorify God.

We were placed on the earth not to chase after personal fulfillment but to glorify God. As we read of the elders in heaven saying, "You are worthy, O Lord, to receive glory and honor and power; for You created all things, and by Your will they exist and were created" (Rev. 4:11), it is a reminder from heaven as to why we are on Earth. We are here to bring glory and pleasure to God. Every day, we should get up and say, "Lord, I am giving my life to You. I am giving this day to You. I am giving my talents to You. How can You use me for Your glory?"

One day, we will be held accountable as Christians for what we did with the opportunities that God gave us. The sad thing is that there will be people in heaven who forever will be in the presence of God, but they will have nothing to show for their lives. Sure, they have been saved. They have been forgiven. They made it to heaven. The problem is that they wasted their opportunities to glorify God on Earth.

In 1 Corinthians 3:13,15, Paul, speaking of this same event regarding the Judgment Seat of Christ, says, "each one's work will become clear; for the Day will declare it, because it will be revealed by fire; and the fire will test each one's work, of what sort it is. If anyone's work is burned, he will suffer loss; but he himself will be saved, yet so as through fire." In other words, some people will make it to heaven, but they will have squandered their lives.

Have you ever seen a sweep at the Oscars where one movie wins all of the awards? I think sometimes we envision heaven as being sort of like the Academy Awards. We expect to hear the name "Billy Graham" and other well-known Christians called frequently. We picture these individuals sweeping up all of the rewards in heaven.

I have no doubt that Billy Graham will receive many rewards for his years of faithful service to God. But I think we will also be in for some surprises in heaven. Imagine, if you will, that you are there in heaven at this awards ceremony when you hear, "And the winner of this award is . . . Maude Firkenbinder!"

Maude Firkenbinder? Who was she? She never preached in a crusade. She never recorded a Christian CD. She never wrote a book. But here is the deal: While Billy Graham was out preaching, Maude was praying. While he was doing his part, Maude was doing hers.

Every one of us is called to do something. Some are called to preach. Others are called to work quietly behind the scenes. Some may reach millions. Others may reach three or four. But in that final day, we will not be held accountable for what God called Billy Graham to do. We will not be held accountable for what God has called our favorite Christian artist to do. We will not be held accountable for what God has called our pastor to do. We will be held accountable for what God has called us to do. Our objective is to be faithful with what God has set before us and to do the best possible job with that. We may not receive many rewards on Earth for our efforts, but we can look forward to them in heaven.

A GOLD-MEDAL FINISH

One of the rewards that will be given in heaven is a crown of righteousness. Paul speaks of it in 2 Timothy 4:

> I have fought the good fight, I have finished the race, I have kept the faith. Finally, there is laid up for me the crown of righteousness, which the Lord, the righteous Judge, will give to me on that Day, and not to me only but also to all who have loved His appearing (vv. 7-8).

This means that if you finish your course and love His appearing, you will have that crown waiting for you. This is what I want to see. I want to see people finish. I rejoice when people make commitments to Christ. But I also rejoice when I see someone finish his or her course well, someone who not only accepted the Lord and was on fire for Him in his or her youth, but who also served the Lord with all the years that God gave. I thank

God when a person like that has crossed the finish line, completing what he or she started.

Friend, this is what I pray for you. I want you to finish the course. This is what God wants for you as well. Finish your course. Love His appearing. There is hope beyond the grave for the believer. That is why we don't have Remember, death is merely a mode of transportation to get us from point *A* to point *B*, and point *B* is heaven. (For more information on this topic of finishing our spiritual race well, see my book *Losers and Winners, Saints and Sinners,* New York: Warner Faith, 2005.)

HOMESICK FOR HEAVEN

Deep down inside, all of us long to be in heaven. It's as though God has built inside of us a homing instinct for heaven. The Bible says that God has placed eternity in our hearts (see Eccles. 3:11). You will have those moments in life when everything is going along beautifully. Perhaps you will be watching a beautiful sunset as you're sitting next to the one you love, and think, *This is so great. I wish it could always be like this.* But it isn't, because it can't be on Earth. Do you know what you are experiencing during moments such as these? It is homesickness for a place you have never seen. It is homesickness for heaven, the future destination of every believer.

That is why you have a longing inside of you that you cannot fill with anything here on Earth. No possession or relationship or experience will ever fill that void. Some people chase after alcohol or drugs, trying to get that high. Others chase after pleasure. But none of these things will do. They are cheap substitutes for the real thing.

You were created to know God. You were created to have a relationship with Him. You were created to go to heaven. And if you have trusted in Christ, one day you will be there.

THE ANTICHRIST, ANTI-SEMITISM AND ARMAGEDDON

AND THEN THE LAWLESS ONE WILL BE REVEALED, WHOM THE
LORD WILL CONSUME WITH THE BREATH OF HIS MOUTH AND
DESTROY WITH THE BRIGHTNESS OF HIS COMING.

2 THESSALONIANS 2:8

The book of Revelation is the unveiling of the future. "Revelation" means "the unveiling," or "to uncover or reveal something that had been previously hidden." We find its origins in the same Greek word from which we get the English word "apocalypse." The book of Revelation is the apocalypse revealed for you. While it is a glimpse into the future, it is also an unveiling of history from God's perspective.

In the first three chapters, Jesus addresses the seven churches of Revelation. Beginning with the church of Ephesus and ending with the church of Laodicea, these chapters speak of three different things:

1. Actual churches that once existed
2. Stages of church history
3. People who would find themselves in the same spiritual condition as the churches to whom Jesus was speaking

When we come to Revelation 4, there is clearly a shift. A very important statement is made in verse 1: "After these things."

After what things? After the things concerning the seven churches.

Revelation 1:19 offers a vital key to understanding this incredible book: "Write the things which you have seen, and the things which are, and the things which will take place after this." In this verse, we see the three divisions of the book of Revelation: "the things which you have seen" (the things God showed and said to John, in Revelation 1); "the things which are" (Church history, given to us in Revelation 2 and 3); and "the things that will take place after this" (*after* the removal, or rapture, of the Church, in Revelation 4).

To summarize, Revelation 1–3 describes the Church. Revelation 4 describes the fact that the Church will be catapulted into the presence of God in eternity. It is a glimpse of what heaven will be like. Then the scene shifts back to Earth, and Revelation 6 describes what the Tribulation period will be like.

A RESTRAINING FORCE

As I have noted, the followers of Jesus Christ have been caught up to meet the Lord in heaven, and then the Tribulation period will begin. The Bible tells us, "For the mystery of lawlessness is already at work; only He who now restrains will do so until He is taken out of the way. And then the lawless one will be revealed" (2 Thess. 2:7-8). When this passage refers to "He who now restrains," it is speaking of the work of the Holy Spirit in the Church.

If you think the world is troubled now, just wait until the Lord takes the true believers—that is, those who have put their faith in Christ—out of it. All hell will break loose, literally. Right now, we, as followers of Jesus, are the restraining force in this world, stopping the spread of evil to a large degree. We stand up and speak for what is true and what is right. But a day is coming when the Lord will call us to be with Him, and then the

Antichrist will emerge and the Tribulation period will begin.

It is essential for us, as Christians, to understand that we will not go through the Tribulation period. According to 1 Thessalonians 5:9, "God did not appoint us to wrath, but to obtain salvation through our Lord Jesus Christ." Some teach that Christians will go through the Tribulation, but I reject that completely. The Tribulation period, especially the last half, will be God's judgment poured out on the world.

Take, for example, two illustrations from Scripture as to why believers will not face this wrath. When God was about to judge Sodom and Gomorrah, did He get His people out first or did He leave them in the wicked cities? He got Lot and his family out first, and then the judgment came. When God was about to bring judgment on the earth through the Flood, did God leave Noah there to drown with everyone else? No, He placed Noah and his family in the ark, where they would be safe.

In the same way, God has not appointed us to receive the wrath that will come upon a wicked world. Speaking to the Church in Revelation 3, Jesus said, "Because you have obeyed my command to persevere, I will protect you from the great time of testing that will come upon the whole world to test those who belong to this world" (v. 10, NLT). In other words, the Lord is saying, "Because you have hung in there and persevered, I will keep you from the Tribulation period."

A COMING WORLD LEADER

Who is this "lawless one" or Antichrist that Paul mentions in 2 Thessalonians 2:7-8, and how will he come on the scene? He will be a charismatic world leader who will emerge with answers to the troubled economy of the world (see Rev. 13:13-18). He will be a man who will bring about a peace treaty, making possible the complete absence of war for three and a half years (see Dan. 9:26-27).

The closest person I could compare him to would be Judas Iscariot. Regarding Judas Iscariot, the Bible says that Satan actually entered his heart (see Luke 22:3). While we know that demons took control of people and entered into them, this is the only time in which we hear that the devil himself entered someone. I am not suggesting that the Antichrist will be the devil incarnate, but he will be about as close as you can possibly come (see Rev. 13:2). He will come as a man of

The Antichrist will come as a man of peace, a man with solutions, and a man who will finally get the Israelis and Palestinians to adhere to a peace treaty.

peace, a man with solutions, and a man who will finally get the Israelis and Palestinians to sign a peace treaty that they actually will adhere to.

Not only will the Antichrist broker this peace treaty, but he also will help the Jews rebuild their long-awaited Temple (see Matt. 24:15; Rev. 11:1). When you travel to Israel today, you find that is the hope of the Jewish people, especially of the religious Jews. They want the Temple erected again. They haven't been able to accomplish this because the Dome of the Rock currently occupies the holy area where the Temple would be rebuilt. The Dome of the Rock is a holy place for Muslims, traditionally believed to be the place where Mohammed ascended to heaven. Therefore, they don't want the Jews rebuilding any Temple anywhere in that vicinity. Whenever a move has been made in that direction, conflict and the threat of a holy war break out.

Somehow, the Antichrist will develop a treaty or solution that will allow the Jews to rebuild their Temple. Many will be so thrilled that they will hail him as the very Messiah (see Rev. 13:4). But after three and a half years, the Bible tells us the Antichrist will show his true colors. Matthew 24:15 calls it the "abomination of desolation." After the Temple has been rebuilt, the Antichrist will erect an image of himself inside, and then will command everyone to worship it (see Dan. 11:31; Rev. 13:14-15). This will mark the halfway point of the Tribulation period.

ANTI-SEMITISM IN THE PAST

This is significant, because gaining people's confidence through economic prosperity and peace has historical precedence. For instance, when Rome came on the scene, it came as a benevolent ruler who would bring peace and economic solutions to a troubled and barbaric world. Yet it was only a matter of time before Rome deified its caesars and demanded them to be worshiped. What started out as a benevolent world power ultimately ended up as a religion. Many Christians lost their lives in the amphitheaters of Rome and in the coliseums, because they would not say, "Caesar is Lord." They stood by their faith in Christ.

Hitler did something very similar when he came on the scene. After World War I, Germany was in desperate financial straits. Inflation was so bad that thousands of people were virtually starving on the streets. Communists were stirring up riots, and there was general chaos. In the midst of this chaos, Hitler began to emerge as the apparent voice of authority. He claimed that Germany would become a people of destiny, that he would be their leader, and that they would have prosperity.

Hitler was sly, because at first he pulled the churches into supporting his agenda. He promised those in the churches that they would not have to fear the Nazis and could still practice their faith freely. But it was only a matter of time before the crosses and Stars of David were replaced by swastikas. As it turned out, Nazism was more than just a philosophy; it was a religious belief imposed upon the people.

Hitler was a prototype of the Antichrist, who came on the scene with benevolent gestures and then revealed himself for who he really was. He had a wicked plan that he called "the final solution." It was his desire to kill every Jewish man, woman and child. He effectively destroyed 6 million Jews in his concentration camps, and probably would have achieved his goal of total elimination of the Jewish race had it not been for his defeat by the Allies.

Jesus, as He spoke of the signs of the last days, said in Luke 21:20, "But when you see Jerusalem surrounded by armies, then know that its desolation is near." This prophecy could not have been fulfilled until somewhat recently, because the Jewish people were scattered around the world. When Jesus gave this prediction, the Jews were still in the land. Although the Romans were ruling over them, there still were Jews in places of authority in Israel. A great dispersion came not long afterward, in which the Jews were scattered to the four corners of the earth. They remained scattered for centuries, although some Jews remained in the land. The Jewish people started to return to the land in the early 1900s, and this trend continued steadily over a period of time.

It wasn't until after the holocaust that the nation of Israel was born. After World War II had ended, the surviving Jews realized that they needed to have their own homeland again. They realized that they couldn't trust another nation to defend them. The holocaust was the catalyst that brought into reality the modern-day miracle of the creation of the nation of Israel. On May 14, 1948, Israel became a nation.

The surrounding Arab states were against this new nation of Israel, but it somehow prevailed with a miniscule army and no sophisticated weapons of war to defend itself. God put His hand on Israel and preserved the people, and they became a nation. We need to be aware that an international focus on Israel is one of the distinctive signs of the last days.

ANTI-SEMITISM IN THE FUTURE

When Jesus spoke of Jerusalem being surround by armies (see Luke 21:20), He was referring to a coming battle, known as the Battle of Armageddon, which will be fought in Israel. It will involve two superpowers: the Antichrist and his 10 confederated nations (see Rev. 17:3,12-13); and the kings of the East, a huge army of millions that will meet in the Valley of Megiddo in Israel (see Rev. 9:16; 16:16). The Battle of Armageddon will be the final war prior to the Second Coming of Jesus Christ. In verse 20, Jesus was saying that when we see Jerusalem surrounded by armies, know that its desolation is near.

Right now, in one sense, Jerusalem is surrounded by armies. All around this tiny nation are hostile enemies that want to see her destroyed. There is almost a global hatred of Israel. For all practical purposes, Israel has only one staunch ally on the face of the earth: the United States of America. And I believe one of the reasons that God has blessed our country is because of our continued support of the Jewish people and their homeland. God made a promise long ago to Abraham and his descendents: "I will bless those who bless you, and I will curse him who curses you; And in you all the families of the earth shall be blessed" (Gen. 12:3).

America has "blessed" Israel by supporting her right to exist and by sending billions of dollars of much-needed support over the years. And God has blessed America. On the other hand, look at the nations that have "cursed" Israel. Great world powers are either now gone or diminished because of their hatred and persecution of the Jewish people.

You would think that people would learn the great lessons of history, but as it has been said, "The only thing we learn from history is we don't learn anything from history." The Antichrist and others will turn the white heat of their anger against the nation of Israel in the last days. God solemnly warns in the book of Zechariah, "And it shall happen in that day that I will make Jerusalem a very heavy stone for all peoples; all who would heave it away will surely be cut in pieces, though all nations of the earth are gathered against it" (Zech. 12:3).

The founder and spiritual leader of the Hamas, who has been behind many of the terrorist attacks against the Israelis over the years, has rejected any ceasefire negotiated between Israel and Palestinian leaders. He has warned that their militants would use "stones, guns, and explosions" to drive the Israelis out of the Middle East.[1] Notice that he did not say, "We just want to live peacefully next to the Israelis, and we fully acknowledge their right to exist." Rather, he said that they want to drive the Israelis out of the Middle East. The late Yasir Arafat was quoted as saying, "We will continue our struggle until a Palestinian boy or a Palestinian girl waves our flag on the walls, mosques, and churches of Jerusalem, the capital of our independent state."[2] Understand, Hamas and the Palestinian Liberation Organization don't just want a homeland; they want Jerusalem. That is the eternal capital of the nation of Israel. It always has been and always will be.

Osama bin Laden has spoken of his desire to see the Israelis removed from the land as well. What is happening in the aftermath of 9/11 is the increased isolation of the nation of Israel, which is only showing us that Bible prophecy is being fulfilled.

Prior to the Battle of Armageddon, there will be an attack on Israel, which is spoken of in Ezekiel 37–39. In Ezekiel, we read about a large force called Magog that will march against Israel (see Ezek. 38:2). Magog was one of Japheth's sons who settled north of the Black Sea in a region we know today as Russia (see Gen. 10:2; 1 Chron. 1:5).

Of course, if you were to look at a world map and note what countries are to the north of Israel today, you will find present-

day Russia among them. Many scholars and students of prophecy believe that Magog is Russia, and I think a pretty good case
could be made for it. It is worth noting there is no great love in
Russia today for the nation of Israel. Fifty-five million of
Russia's 250 million people are Muslim, most of whom at best
do not support the Jewish people or their homeland and at
worst oppose it.

Ezekiel says that Magog will march with her allies, one of
them being Persia. Ancient Persia has become what we know
today as Iran. There is a lot of concern about Iran's development
of nuclear weapons. One of its leaders even spoke publicly about
the possibility of a nuclear exchange with Israel.

In 2005, Iranian President Mahmoud Ahmadinejad declared
in a speech to thousands of students gathered at the World
Without Zionism conference that Israel is a "disgraceful blot"
that should be "wiped off the map." Ahmadinejad's words set a
hard-line foreign policy course at odds with that of his moderate
predecessor and underscored the U.S. government's concern
over Iran's nuclear weapons program. Ahmadinejad also condemned Iran's neighbors for seeking to build new relations with
the nation of Israel. "Anybody who recognizes Israel will burn in
the fire of the Islamic nation's fury," he was quoted as saying.[3]

Ahmadinejad's speech came hours before a Palestinian suicide bomber blew himself up in the Israeli town of Hadera,
killing five people. "There is no doubt that the new wave in
Palestine will soon wipe off this disgraceful blot from the face of
the Islamic world," the Iranian president said regarding these
bomb attacks in Israel. Iran aids several militant Palestinian
groups (such as Hamas and Islamic Jihad) and provides support
and training through proxies to Lebanese Hezbollah guerrillas.[4]

Ethiopia is mentioned in Ezekiel 38:5. Once part of the
Communist block, Ethiopia is a very strong Muslim nation
today, as is Libya, another nation specifically mentioned as an

ally of Magog. Libya has long been a sponsor of terrorism and has been dedicated to the destruction of Israel.

Isn't it interesting when you think about how the Jews are back in the land again? Isn't it interesting to note that to her extreme north is Russia, which has hostility toward Israel? Isn't it interesting that all of Magog's allies that are mentioned in Ezekiel are largely Muslim and would love to see Israel destroyed? This is exactly what the Bible said would happen. In Ezekiel 38, God, speaking to the enemies of Israel, said:

> At that time evil thoughts will come to your mind, and you will devise a wicked scheme. You will say, "Israel is an unprotected land filled with unwalled villages! I will march against her and destroy these people who live in such confidence! I will go to those once-desolate cities that are again filled with people who have returned from exile in many nations. I will capture vast amounts of plunder and take many slaves, for the people are rich with cattle now, and they think the whole world revolves around them!" (vv. 10-12, *NLT*).

It may not seem that Israel lives in confidence today, but actually, she does. For a long time, Israel has had nuclear capabilities. All of her enemies know this well and it has kept them at bay. Her enemies fear her and know that Israel probably has the most effective military fighting force, man-for-man, on the planet. All things considered, Israel lives in confidence today, just as this passage says. However, this large force known as Magog eventually will invade her. According to Scripture, this cannot happen until the following takes place:

1. Israel has to be scattered and regathered as a nation. *Check.*

2. There has to be a strong, hostile nation to the north of Israel that could potentially invade her. *Check.*
3. Israel has to be dwelling with security and confidence. *Check.*
4. Israel has to be isolated from the other nations of the world. This hasn't quite happened yet. Israel still has the United States as her ally.

I fully expect that in the days ahead, the United States will abandon Israel as an ally. The invasion of Israel could happen sometime soon.

I fully expect that in the days ahead, the United States will abandon Israel as an ally. When Israel is isolated, she will be in this vulnerable place Scripture speaks of. As you can see, the invasion of Israel could happen sometime soon.

DIVINE INTERVENTION

How will God react to this invasion? According to Ezekiel 38, He will personally step in and defend her:

> "And it will come to pass at the same time, when Gog comes against the land of Israel," says the Lord GOD, "that My fury will show in My face. For in My jealousy and in the fire of My wrath I have spoken: 'Surely in that day there shall be a great earthquake in the land of Israel, so that the fish of the sea, the birds of the heavens, the beasts of the field, all creeping things that creep on the earth, and all men who are on the face of the earth shall shake at My presence. The mountains shall be thrown down, the steep places shall fall, and every wall shall fall to the ground.' I will call for a sword against Gog throughout all My mountains," says the Lord God. "Every man's sword

will be against his brother. And I will bring him to judgment with pestilence and bloodshed; I will rain down on him, on his troops, and on the many peoples who are with him, flooding rain, great hailstones, fire, and brimstone. . . . Then they shall know that I am the LORD" (vv. 18-23).

After Magog attacks Israel, the United States won't save her. In fact, Israel won't even be able to save herself. God says that He will supernaturally step in, turn back this invading army and then judge them. The result will be a nationwide revival in the land of Israel, the land of the Bible (see Rom. 11:25-32).

It is important to understand that modern Israel today is largely a secular nation. Sure, there are many religious Jews who live there and practice their faith, but the average Israeli is not a person of faith. But after this divine intervention on God's part, many of the people will turn back to the God of Abraham, Isaac and Jacob. They will turn to Jesus as the Messiah, and God will pour out His Spirit on the nation of Israel again.

The Bible says that in the aftermath of this battle, the weapons will be burned for seven years (see Ezek. 39:9). Therefore, it seems to me that the invasion of Magog against Israel will come in close proximity to the Tribulation, which also is a seven-year period. I can't imagine the weapons of this war to continue being burned into the millennial reign of Christ, when He comes and establishes His kingdom on this earth. My point is, this invasion of Israel that Ezekiel prophesies could happen very soon.

WATCH THE SIGNS

So what does this all mean to us? Anytime you see any hostility toward Israel, anytime you see her become more isolated from the other nations of the world, anytime you hear talk of the

Jewish Temple being rebuilt, pay attention. These are supersigns of the end times.

As I have already mentioned, before God will pour out His Spirit on Israel, the Church must be removed. Romans 11:25 says, "Blindness in part has happened to Israel until the fullness of the Gentiles has come in." Over most Jewish people today, there is a spiritual blindness in which they are not all that open to hearing about Jesus as their Messiah. God says that He will lift the blinders. But before He does this and pours out His Spirit upon the Jews, the full gathering of the Gentiles must take place. To put it another way, before God can pour out His Spirit on Israel, He must take the Church out of the way.

So when I see any hostility toward Israel, when I see her become more isolated from the rest of the world, it serves as a reminder that the Lord's return is close. The Antichrist cannot be revealed until the Church is taken. The Spirit of God cannot be poured out upon Israel until the Church is taken.

As I see in our world today these movements toward a global economy, toward the isolation of Israel, toward one world religion, and toward one world leader, it says to me that Jesus is coming back very, very soon.

Notes

1. Kelley, Jack, "Hamas Leader Refuses to Accept Cease-Fire Agreement," *USA Today*, October 18, 2000, p. 14A.
2. Yassir Arafat, addressing a Fatah conference in Ramallah, March 19, 1999. Quoted in "Palestinian Leadership Renews Calls for Violence," *The Middle East Media Research Institute*, Special Dispatch Series No. 29, March 22, 1999.
3. Nasser Karimi, "Iran Leader Call's for Israel's Destruction," Associated Press, October 26, 2005. Online version at http://www.twincities.com/mld/twincities/13000779.htm (accessed November 7, 2005).
4. Ibid.

ABSENT AMERICA

"It was the best of times, it was the worst of times . . ." So begins Charles Dickens's classic *A Tale of Two Cities*. The same thing could be said of the times in which we are living. But sadly, it will even get worse. Much worse.

Yes, hard times are coming for Planet Earth. We are going to see ecological disaster on a scale never before known to man. Unprecedented famine, disease and, quite possibly, nuclear war will sweep the planet and culminate in the war to end all wars, the Battle of Armageddon. Millions of people will lose their lives as Satan has his heyday on the planet. Those who would have us cast off moral constraints, those who do not want to live by the standards God has set down in His Word for our protection, will finally have their way—at least for a time.

As I mentioned earlier, once the Church is removed as the restraining force on Earth, Satan will be able to do what he has wanted to do for a long time. While we see great wickedness in our world now, it will only get increasingly worse, culminating in the war to end all wars. Were it not for the intervention of God Himself, no one would survive.

One thing that is of great interest to me, and also is of great concern, is the apparent absence in Bible prophecy of the reigning superpower in the world today, the United States. As we look at the key players in what will be the Battle of Armageddon, it is interesting to note the nations the Bible mentions as being active in the last days: Persia (modern-day Iran) is mentioned.

Libya and Ethiopia are mentioned specifically as well. Russia is quite possibly referred to, as well as China. And of course, the nation of Israel is mentioned. But the one nation strangely absent from the list is the only true superpower left on the face of the earth: the United States of America. Where is the United States? Why are we not in the last-days scenario?

THE FOUR HORSEMEN OF THE APOCALYPSE

Before we explore some possible answers to that question, let's take a brief look into the future, as described in Revelation 6. This chapter in Revelation provides an overview of the most difficult and devastating times that our planet will ever experience, the Great Tribulation period. It will be God's final countdown for humanity before the personal, visible return of Jesus Christ to the earth. The Tribulation period will be such a severe time that it will be unparalleled in world history and never will be equaled again. Speaking of this time in Matthew 24, Jesus said:

> For that will be a time of greater horror than anything the world has ever seen or will ever see again. In fact, unless that time of calamity is shortened, the entire human race will be destroyed. But it will be shortened for the sake of God's chosen ones (vv. 21-22, NLT).

This period is symbolized by what we call the four horsemen of the Apocalypse, who come with varying degrees of deception, war and plague.

The First Horseman
The first horseman rides a white horse:

> As I watched, the Lamb broke the first of the seven seals on the scroll. Then one of the four living beings called

out with a voice that sounded like thunder, "Come!" I looked up and saw a white horse. Its rider carried a bow, and a crown was placed on his head. He rode out to win many battles and gain the victory (Rev. 6:1-2).

If you've ever watched an old western, you know that if someone rides a white horse or wears a white hat, he is usually the good guy. On the other hand, if he rides a black horse and wears a black hat, he is usually the bad guy. But in the case of this first horseman in verse 2, there is an interesting twist. Although it appears that the rider on the white horse is the hero, in realty he is the villain. This rider, the first horseman of the Apocalypse, is none other then the Antichrist himself.

Because this rider is on a white horse, he is sometimes confused with another rider on a white horse mentioned in Revelation 19:11. This later reference, however, speaks of Jesus Christ. The false Christ, the Antichrist, mentioned in Revelation 6:2 wears a crown, while in Revelation 19, Jesus, the rider on the white horse, wears many crowns. In the original language, the word "crown" used in Revelation 6:2 speaks of someone who is conquering. In contrast, the word used for the crowns worn by Jesus in Revelation 19 speaks of royalty.

As I mentioned in the last chapter, when the Antichrist comes on the scene, he initially looks like a charismatic and visionary world leader. He brings solutions to the economic woes of the world. But ultimately, he shows his true colors. Remember, he will be successful in brokering a peace treaty between the Israelis and Palestinians that they will live by for a period of time. He will help the Jews rebuild their Temple, and some will even herald him as the Messiah of Israel. But at the halfway point of the Tribulation period, the Antichrist will commit what is called the "abomination of desolation" (see Matt. 24:15). He will erect an image of himself in the rebuilt

Jewish Temple and will command people everywhere to worship him.

You might be wondering why anyone would ever consider submitting to such a thing. But we need to realize that by this time, the Antichrist will have established a new system of trade that will have effectively done away with cash. All financial transactions will be done by some type of electronic transfer. The way that this will be done is by a mark people take, as mentioned in Revelation 13:

> He causes all, both small and great, rich and poor, free and slave, to receive a mark on their right hand or on their foreheads, and that no one may buy or sell except one who has the mark or the name of the beast, or the number of his name. Here is wisdom. Let him who has understanding calculate the number of the beast, for it is the number of a man: His number is 666 (vv. 16-18).

Will people literally be walking around with three numbers on their foreheads or right hands? Not necessarily. Remember, the apostle John was speaking from a first-century perspective. It was almost as though God had put him in a spiritual time machine and catapulted him into the twenty-first century. In first-century language, he was trying to describe things that are commonplace to us now.

Imagine how futuristic and unbelievable this might have sounded to people 500 years ago, much less 2000 years ago. But does this sound like a stretch today? No. We can envision this happening right now. Before computers became such a vital part of our lives, it was hard to imagine how this prophecy could be fulfilled, but no longer. In our generation alone, we have seen the development of the technology that would be necessary for one person to have total economic control. We have methods of transmitting data through satellite technology and, of course, we have the World Wide Web.

In our post-9/11 nation, there are tighter controls and more freedom given to government agencies to monitor, eavesdrop and get the information that they need when they need it. Because we all so desperately want national security, we are willing to give up some personal freedoms.

There has been talk of a national ID card, where key personal data could be placed on a tiny microchip in a plastic card that U.S. citizens would be required to carry at all times. Of course, the problem with this is that people can lose their ID cards, just like they can lose their purses or wallets. How much easier it would be to somehow place that information inside a person in the form of a little pellet or microchip. Can you see how something like this could be rationalized?

In our generation alone, we have seen the development of the technology that would be necessary for one person to have total economic control.

The technology certainly is available. On a visit to the veterinarian's office with my dog, I noticed a sign advertising an ID implant for animals. When I asked what this was, I was told that it is a little implant about the size of a grain of rice that holds data. It could be inserted right under my dog's skin. If I lost my dog, he could be scanned to find out to whom he belonged.

Will this technology be applied to humans next? It already has happened. On May 10, 2002, in Boca Raton, Florida, Jeffrey and Leslie Jacobs, along with their son, Derek, became the first people in the world to be implanted with a VeriChip, made by Applied Digital Solutions.[1] The family, nicknamed "the Chipsons," wanted to be implanted with the VeriChip to allow easy access to their medical and emergency data, and because of security concerns. Leslie Jacobs said, "I have nothing to hide, so I wouldn't mind having the chip for verification. I already have an ID card, so why not have a chip?"[2]

I believe that things like this help us to see how close we could be to the very scenario described in the prophecies of Scripture. Don't get me wrong—I am not saying that a national ID card is the mark of the Beast that Revelation 13 speaks of. What I am saying is that I find it interesting how we are moving toward this type of thing not only nationally but also internationally. I bring it up as a point of interest to say that we are beginning to see Bible prophecy fulfilled before our very eyes. If the emergence of the Antichrist is getting close, then the return of Jesus Christ is even closer.

Historian Arnold Toynbee said, "By forcing on mankind more and more lethal weapons and at the same time making the world more and more interdependent economically, technology has brought mankind to such a degree of distress that we are ripe for the deifying of any new Caesar who might succeed in giving the world unity and peace."[3]

Toynbee was right.

That "Caesar" he warned of will be the Antichrist who will harness the latest technology for his wicked ends.

The Second Horseman

Returning to the four horseman of Revelation 6, we read that the next horseman, riding a red horse, will bring war:

> When He opened the second seal, I heard the second living creature saying, "Come and see." Another horse, fiery red, went out. And it was granted to the one who sat on it to take peace from the earth, and that people should kill one another; and there was given to him a great sword (vv. 3-4).

After the Antichrist harnesses the economic and military system, he will play his hand and show his true colors. War will break out. Notice from the above verses that the horse is fiery red. In Revelation 12:3, Satan is described as "a great, fiery red dragon." The devil will be behind the war that breaks out, because he hates humanity. He loves global destruction. He delights in the senseless slaughter of people. Satan, though he cannot become a human being, will bestow his power on a person, and that person will be the Antichrist. If Satan ever had a son, the Antichrist would be him.

It is important for you to understand that the devil is behind the wars and struggles on this planet. When you see horrific tragedies like those of 9/11, as you recall the atrocities by the Nazis in World War II against the Jews and others, as you look at many of the other senseless and wicked things that have gone on in this world, then you have to know that there is a devil. Even man at his worst is not capable of some of the horrific things that we have seen in our world. Yes, there is a devil, and he is behind these atrocities.

This planet has seen some horrible wars throughout its history. In World War I, more than 10 million people lost their lives. It was thought to be the "War that would end all wars," but it only took 20 years for a new and even more terrible war to develop. During World War II, almost 50 million people died.

But these wars, as horrible as they were, will be nothing compared to the scale of war that will be unleashed by Satan during the Tribulation period. Today, we have weapons of mass destruction. The United States and several other nations are bona fide members of what they call the "nuclear club." But smaller, rogue nations have obtained these weapons of mass destruction as well.

Currently, humanity has the capacity to fulfill what is predicted in Revelation 6. There are at least 60,000 hydrogen bombs in the world today, enough nuclear firepower to destroy the world 17 times over in a blinding flash.

Did you know that the Soviet Union had 30,000 atomic or neutron warheads at the time it collapsed, many of which were aimed at population centers? Since the breakup of what President Reagan once called the "Evil Empire, " no one knows what has happened to all those weapons.

At the time of its collapse, Russia claimed that it was too poor to dismantle the warheads in Yugoslavia and other struggling republics. Since the host countries could not afford to man them, dismantle them or keep them from terrorists, these cash-poor countries began to sell them to rogue nations. Over 10,000 nuclear scientists from Russia are reported to have migrated with these warheads to other countries. A case could be made that the world is in a much more precarious condition today then when the Soviet Communists controlled all their weapons!

Conventional thinking has long been that the superpowers keep each other at bay. This is called the M A D.D. theory. Basically, in a nutshell, this theory states that if you nuke us, we will nuke you. For all practical purposes, this theory has worked—that is, until now. Today, we face a new kind of enemy.

As horrible as the Nazis were in World War II, they were an enemy that we could fight on a battlefield. As horrible as the Japanese attack on Pearl Harbor was, we knew where the attackers came from and how to find them. But today there is a new enemy that strikes and then hides in caves.

These individuals are not insane madmen, but clever, well-organized and deadly terrorists. They hate America, they hate Christianity, and they hate Israel. This is clearly seen in their rhetoric. Osama bin Laden was quoted as saying, "The new Jewish crusader campaign is led by the biggest crusader Bush under the banner of the cross."[4] This new enemy our world faces is devilish. These individuals are willing to die for their twisted beliefs and to take as many people with them as possible.

One scientist was recently asked which weapons would be used in World War III. "I'm not sure exactly which weapons will be detonated in World War III," he said, "But I'll tell you which ones will be used in World War IV . . . rocks. Rocks will be all that's left if World War III ever takes place."

This may have sounded incomprehensible 100 years ago, but not any more. Today, this could be the fallout and result of a nuclear exchange. But then again it could be cataclysmic. A few eruptions the size of Mount Saint Helens or a few earthquakes and tsunamis on the scale of the Southeast Asia quake of 2004 and you would be right where the Bible says. So we see how quickly the events of Revelation 6 could begin to unfold.

The Third Horseman

Following the red horse, the next horseman of the Apocalypse will ride a black horse:

> When He opened the third seal, I heard the third living creature say, "Come and see." So I looked, and behold, a black horse, and he who sat on it had a pair of scales in his hand. And I heard a voice in the midst of the four living creatures saying, "A quart of wheat for a denarius, and three quarts of barley for a denarius; and do not harm the oil and the wine" (Rev. 6:5-6).

This is a description of global famine. Scientists have predicted that, in the aftermath of a nuclear war, the world's food supply would be affected. These verses possibly could be describing such a condition, giving you an idea of the radioactivity that would be present after the detonation of nuclear weapons.

The Fourth Horseman

Next, a pale horse appears:

> When He opened the fourth seal, I heard the voice of the fourth living creature saying, "Come and see." So I looked, and behold, a pale horse. And the name of him who sat on it was Death, and Hades followed with him. And power was given to them over a fourth of the earth, to kill with sword, with hunger, with death, and by the beasts of the earth (Rev. 6:7-8).

Paralleling these verses is a statement by Jesus in Luke 21: "Nation will rise against nation, and kingdom against kingdom. And there will be great earthquakes in various places, and famines and pestilences; and there will be fearful sights and great signs from heaven" (vv 10-11) This would have sounded futuristic 100 years ago, but not today. With biological warfare a reality, it makes prophecies like these appear quite plausible.

THE WAR TO END ALL WARS

As mentioned in the previous chapter, world history as we know it will ultimately end in the land of Israel in a valley known as Megiddo at the Battle of Armageddon. Revelation tells us that a massive superpower, or superpowers, known as the kings of the East, will march through the dried-up Euphrates River to meet the combined forces of the Antichrist to fight this war to end all wars (see Rev. 16:12-16).

Who are the kings of the East, and who are the confederated nations behind Antichrist? We can only speculate. Many believe "the kings of the East" might be a reference to China. These kings will field an army of two hundred million (see Rev. 9:16). Is there a nation on Earth that could do that? Only one, as a matter of fact, and that nation is China.

With a population of more than one billion, China announced in 1997 that it could raise an army of 352 million soldiers. This means that China could send 200 million to fight in the battle of Armageddon and still have 152 million left to defend its homeland. When John wrote these words, there were not even 200 million people on the face of the earth. This is something that could only happen in the last days. Thus, while we can't be certain that China is "the kings of the East" mentioned in Revelation, it is noteworthy that China has the ability to field an army of that size.

> **While we can't be certain that China is "the kings of the East" mentioned in Revelation, it is noteworthy that China has the ability to field an army of that size.**

Many believe the 10 nations unified under the Antichrist will come out of what we know as the European Union today. This may be the case, or this may change before this scenario unfolds.

WHERE DID AMERICA GO?

But I want to come back to the question I raised at the beginning of this chapter: Where is the United States in all of this? Why is it that we can read of relatively small nations like Iraq, Iran and Libya in Bible prophecy and can possibly find China and Russia, but we cannot find the United States of America? I want to offer three plausible answers.

Nuclear War

Perhaps the United States is not mentioned in Scripture because it will be devastated by a nuclear war. It is a horrible scenario and one that none of us would want to even imagine, but there are no guarantees that this could not happen. Frankly, the possibility has never been greater. Some would think that because the Cold War is over, the threat is gone. But many nations have nuclear weapons. A rogue nation with nuclear capabilities (or even a terrorist group) could set off a chain of events that would lead to such devastation. I hope this isn't the case, but we simply cannot rule it out.

A Decline as a World Power

As our country becomes more and more secular, systematically eliminating God and His Word from our government, judicial system, educational system and the arts, we will begin to reap the inevitable results of sin and will begin to rot from the inside out. Historian Will Durant pointed out that a great nation is not destroyed from the outside until it has first fallen apart on the inside. Certainly, we can see the moral decay in the United States today.

The Bible says, "Righteousness exalts a nation, but sin is a reproach to any people" (Prov. 14:34). If we forget God and abandon His Word, we will reap the inevitable results of sin. To some degree, we already are—we see the breakdown of the family, rampant crime, and so many other problems today that have come from disobeying God.

A Great Revival Takes Place

There is one more possibility that I find a lot more hopeful. I think you will too. In this scenario, a great revival takes place in the United States. If the United States were to have a revival, it would have a far-reaching impact when the Rapture occurred.

Think about it—the United States has a population today of approximately 285 million. Although some polls have suggested that there are approximately 140 million Christians in America today, let's be realistic and suppose that 25 percent of all Americans today are believers. This would mean that the United States has a population of some 75 million true believers.

When the Rapture occurs, don't you think this would have an impact on our country if 75 million people disappeared? Imagine what would happen if people in every level of government, the military, the economic and business community, agriculture, medicine and communications suddenly disappeared from the face of the Earth. It undoubtedly would have a crippling effect on our nation's entire infrastructure. Of course, once the Rapture has taken place, every nation will be affected. Think about that for a moment. This could be the explanation as to why the Bible does not mention United States in prophecies concerning the last days. Needless to say, I prefer this scenario.

I would only hope and pray that we will have some kind of revival in America and that our nation will turn to the Lord on a scale such as never has been known before. This is what we need to pray for in our country today. We, as the Church, need to do what we do best: pray and preach the gospel. We really need God in the United States today.

The future appears quite bleak. What gives me some sense of optimism, some kind of hope, is the knowledge that a revival could come to America. This has long been my prayer, and I would so love to see it—to see the people of our nation turn back to God. That is our only hope.

Notes

1. Jim Goldman, "Meet 'The Chipsons,'" *ABC News*, May 10, 2002. http://abcnews.go.com/sections/scitech/TechTV/techtv_chipfamily020510.htm l (accessed May 2002).
2. Julia Scheeres, "They Want Their ID Chips Now," *Wired News*, February 6, 2002. http://www.wired.com/news/print/0,1294,50187,00.html (accessed September 2005).

3. A. J. Toynbee, quoted in J. Vernon McGee, *Revelation: Chapters 6—13* (Nashville, TN: Thomas Nelson, 1995), n.p.

4. Osama bin Laden, quoted on "Online News Hour," *Public Broadcasting Station,* September 24, 2001. http://www.pbs.org/newshour/bb/military/terroristat tack/binladen-letter_9-24.html (accessed November 2005).

HEAVEN ON EARTH

CHAPTER 6

BEHOLD, HE IS COMING WITH CLOUDS, AND EVERY EYE WILL SEE HIM.

REVELATION 1:7

Newspapers have a certain type they save only for the mega news events. It is used for those screaming headlines that are about two to three times larger than the headlines you would usually see on the front page. This kind of type was used when Pearl Harbor was bombed. It was used when John F. Kennedy was shot. It was used on September 11, 2001. This exclusive type has been given a very significant name: Second Coming. I find that remarkable. It isn't called Big News type or Major Event type. It is called Second Coming type. Even the hardened news media, which has covered every kind of story imaginable, realizes that there never will be a bigger event globally than the Second Coming of Jesus Christ.

More than 300 passages in the Bible address the subject of Christ's return. When Jesus walked this earth, He referred to it many times, as in Matthew 24 when He said, "Immediately after the tribulation of those days the sun will be darkened. . . . Then the sign of the Son of Man will appear in heaven, and then all the tribes of the earth will mourn, and they will see the Son of Man coming on the clouds of heaven with power and great glory" (vv. 29-30).

THREE THINGS TO CONSIDER ABOUT THE SECOND COMING

There are three important points that we need to realize from this and other statements in Scripture about the return of Jesus.

First, when Jesus comes back, it will be public and seen by all. There will be no mistaking it when it happens. It is not as though someone will say the next day, "Did Christ come back last night, or was that just a radical storm?" The Bible says, "For as the lightning comes from the east and flashes to the west, so also will the coming of the Son of Man be" (Matt. 24:27).

The Bible predicts that in the last days there will be cult-like groups that will claim Christ has returned and revealed Himself to them or that a certain person is Jesus who has come back to the earth. Jesus Himself warned that there will be people who will make statements like these: "So if someone tells you, 'Look, the Messiah is out in the desert,' don't bother to go and look. Or, 'Look, he is hiding here,' don't believe it!" (Matt. 24:26, *NLT*). Trust me, people will definitely know when Christ returns.

Second, Jesus will come immediately after the Tribulation period (see Matt. 24:29-30). Jesus will bring this very dark time on the planet to a close. As the Battle of Armageddon is in full swing, Christ will visibly and physically return to the earth to establish His kingdom.

Third, Jesus' return will be accompanied by sadness and weeping. Zechariah 12:10 says, "Then they will look on Me whom they pierced. Yes, they will mourn for Him as one mourns for his only son, and grieve for Him as one grieves for a firstborn." The world will realize that this indeed was the Messiah, and they missed it. There will be great weeping, because it will be too late then. This time, Christ will return in judgment to execute righteousness and justice on the earth:

Now I saw heaven opened, and behold, a white horse. And He who sat on him was called Faithful and True, and in righteousness He judges and makes war. His eyes were like a flame of fire, and on His head were many crowns. He had a name written that no one knew except Himself. He was clothed with a robe dipped in blood, and His name is called The Word of God. And the armies in heaven, clothed in fine linen, white and clean, followed Him on white horses (Rev. 19:11-14).

This is the big event. When Jesus came to Earth the first time, people were expecting Him to come in this manner. They expected the Messiah to come in power and glory. Although the Bible teaches this, it also reaches that the Messiah first would come to suffer for the sin of the world. So when Christ came the first time, instead of coming in the clouds, He was born in a humble Bethlehem stable to Mary and Joseph. He walked this earth for 33 years and ultimately went to the cross and was tortured and murdered for the sins of the world.

The first time Jesus came to Earth, He came in humility. The next time, He will come in glory.

Because Jesus' disciples believed that He would establish His earthly kingdom then and there, they thought things had gone awry when Jesus was arrested and crucified. It was only later that they realized He was born to die so that we might live. He came for the purpose of dying on the cross. The Bible says, "So Christ was offered once to bear the sins of many. To those who eagerly wait for Him He will appear a second time, apart from sin, for salvation" (Heb. 9:28).

The first time Jesus came to Earth, He came in humility. The next time, He will come in glory. When Jesus had finished His ministry of being crucified and resurrected from the dead, He ascended up into heaven. As the disciples watched Him leave, two angels said to them, "Men of Galilee, why are you standing here staring at the sky? Jesus has been taken away from you into heaven. And someday, just as you saw him go, he will return!" (Acts 1:11, *NLT*).

HEAVEN'S ARMIES

When Christ returns, He also will bring armies of saints with Him (see Rev. 19:14). Enoch mentioned these armies as well. According to Jude:

> Now Enoch, the seventh from Adam, prophesied about these men also, saying, "Behold, the Lord comes with ten thousands of His saints, to execute judgment on all, to convict all who are ungodly among them of all their ungodly deeds which they have committed in an ungodly way, and of all the harsh things which ungodly sinners have spoken against Him" (vv. 14-15).

Who are these saints who will make up this heavenly army? Colossians 3:4 gives us the answer: "When Christ who is our life appears, then you also will appear with Him in glory." It will be the ultimate Holy Land tour, led by Jesus Christ Himself. Although Christians will be caught up to heaven in the Rapture, we will return with Christ to the earth in the Second Coming. As it has been said, "That which goes up must come down." We will come back with the Lord when He establishes His kingdom on Earth and reigns for 1,000 years.

So, not only will we return with Jesus Christ in the Second Coming, but we also will reign with Him, according to Revelation 20:4:

> And I saw thrones, and they sat on them, and judgment was committed to them. Then I saw the souls of those who had been beheaded for their witness to Jesus and for the word of God, who had not worshiped the beast or his image, and had not received his mark on their foreheads or on their hands. And they lived and reigned with Christ for a thousand years.

Over whom will we reign? There will be survivors of the Tribulation period who will be alive for the millennial reign of Christ. And as improbable as it may seem, there will be unbelievers during the millennium (possibly descendants of Tribulation survivors) who will be part of one final rebellion at the end of the millennium (see Rev. 20:7-9).

When Jesus taught the disciples to pray "Our Father in heaven, hallowed be Your name. Your kingdom come. Your will be done on earth as it is in heaven" (Matt. 6:9-10), He was showing us that we should look forward to the day when He will rule as King of kings and Lord of lords. There will be no more corruption, no more terrorism, no more war. Everything will change. Then—and only then—will there be peace.

When the angels announced the arrival of Jesus in Bethlehem to the shepherds keeping watch over their flocks, they said, "Glory to God in the highest, and on earth peace, goodwill toward men!" (Luke 2:14). A more literal translation of the statement the angels made would be "Glory to God in the highest, and peace on earth among men, with whom God is well pleased."

The problem is that we aren't pleasing God. The problem is that we are not obeying the laws and truths of God. The problem is that, as a human race, we have turned from God. This is where the wars and conflicts come from. As James 4:1 says, "What is causing the quarrels and fights among you? Isn't it the whole army of evil desires at war within you?" (*NLT*). It is our own selfish natures that cause us to war and fight, and as a result, we are in constant conflict.

IN PURSUIT OF PEACE

From the beginning of time, humanity has wanted for peace. We have joined peace movements. We have marched for peace. We have gone to war for peace. We have given prizes for peace. Some people urge us through messages on their bumper stickers to visualize world peace, and then they cut us off on the freeway. People can try to visualize peace all they want, but no group of people and no politician ever will bring world peace.

Sure, the Antichrist will bring his pseudo-peace, but it will not be real or lasting. However, this event of the Second Coming—and this event only—will bring an end to the senseless killing and wars of mankind. As honorable as the intentions of our government and our allies may be, we never will be able to effectively eradicate terrorism from the face of the earth. We never will be able to stop all wars and conflicts with military or political solutions. This will only happen when the Creator Himself returns and repossesses what is rightfully His. Hanging over this war-weary planet will be a new sign that reads, "Under new management."

That day is coming. Let's read about it.

> Then I saw an angel come down from heaven with the key to the bottomless pit and a heavy chain in his hand. He seized the dragon—that old serpent, the Devil, Satan—and bound him in chains for a thousand years. The angel threw him into the bottomless pit, which he then shut and locked so Satan could not deceive the nations anymore until the thousand years were finished. Afterward he would be released again for a little while (Rev. 20:1-3, NLT).

The word "millennium" means one thousand. When we refer to the reign of Christ, we often call it the millennial reign or the millennium. It is during this time that Jesus will establish His kingdom on Earth. The first thing that He will do is lock up Satan (I am really looking forward to this day).

Long ago, Satan lost his high-ranking position in heaven because of his rebellion against God. He was once Lucifer (the "shining one"), a powerful, high-ranking angel, possibly on the level of Michael (an archangel) or Gabriel. The problem was that he wanted the top job. He didn't want to worship God; he wanted to be worshiped as though he were God. He wanted to be God Himself (see Isa. 14:12-15).

At the Second Coming of Christ, Satan's ultimate day of humbling will come. Although for years he has been at the top of the heap of demon powers, an angel will bind him in chains (see Rev. 20:2). Obviously, God could have done this earlier, but according to His plan and purpose, this issue of rebellion had to be fully tested. It had to run its course. It had to be shown clearly to all the universe that no one has the power to govern apart from God.

Prior to the Second Coming, Satan will have all of the hosts of the fallen angels, the demons, the Antichrist, and the false prophet, together with the world of unbelievers, under his control:

> **I have seen rational, clear-thinking people do the craziest things under the power of sin. It usually begins with a little compromise.**

"All the world marveled at this miracle and followed the beast in awe. They worshiped the dragon for giving the beast such power, and they worshiped the beast" (Rev. 13:3-4, *NLT*). We know "the beast" mentioned in these verses is the Antichrist, and "the dragon" is Satan. Everyone will worship this world leader and the devil who gave him his power.

This should serve as a reminder to us of how deceiving sin can be. I have seen rational, clear-thinking people do the craziest things under the power of sin. It usually begins with a little compromise.

As a young boy, I loved to light plastic toy army men on fire. Don't ask me why. I would take the little figures that were holding their rifles and light the tip of the rifles. Much to my delight, they would start to melt. One night, I happened to be engaging in this junior pyromania with my little soldiers on newspaper. Of course, the whole paper quickly went up in flames. I grabbed all of the burning papers and threw them into a wastebasket, which unfortunately, was made of rattan. It too ignited. So I picked up everything and threw it in the sink. Fortunately, I was able to put out the fire. What started out small ended up big.

In the same way, no one plans to fall big-time into sin. They start playing with sin and flirting with it, mistakenly thinking that they can control it. But soon, it becomes a problem that is out of control. That is how sin works. It deceives you.

When Christ takes control of the world and Satan is bound, the world finally will be at peace. Isaiah described what the world will be like during the Lord's millennial reign: "The Lord will settle international disputes. All the nations will beat their swords into plowshares and their spears into pruning hooks. All wars will stop, and military training will come to an end" (Isa. 2:4, *NLT*).

PARADISE FOUND

No more war. No more depression. No more disabilities. No more wheelchairs or crutches. No more blindness or deafness. There will be joy and happiness. I love the picture the Bible paints of what this world will be like:

And when he comes, he will open the eyes of the blind and unstop the ears of the deaf. The lame will leap like a deer, and those who cannot speak will shout and sing! Springs will gush forth in the wilderness, and streams will water the desert. The parched ground will become a pool, and springs of water will satisfy the thirsty land. Marsh grass and reeds and rushes will flourish where desert jackals once lived. And a main road will go through that once deserted land. It will be named the

Highway of Holiness. Evil-hearted people will never travel on it. It will be only for those who walk in God's ways; fools will never walk there (Isa. 35:5-8, *NLT*).

The curse that has been on the world because of sin will be lifted when Christ comes to rule and reign. Those who have disabilities will be in the new bodies that God has created for them. As Romans 8:19 tells us, "For all creation is waiting eagerly for that future day when God will reveal who his children really are" (*NLT*). God has a new world for us, and it will be glorious.

One of the things about this new world, according to Scripture, will be a subdued animal kingdom. Isaiah tells us, "The wolf also shall dwell with the lamb, the leopard shall lie down with the young goat, the calf and the young lion and the fatling together; and a little child shall lead them" (Isa. 11:6). This will happen during the millennial reign of Christ. Zoos and wild animal parks will no longer be necessary, because these animals will roam free. As an animal lover, I am looking forward to that.

A number of years ago, I went to Africa. It was so amazing to be out in the open plains with wild animals everywhere. On a drive through a game preserve, we drove right up to a pride of lions. I asked our guide what would happen if we climbed out of the truck.

"The lions would kill you," he replied, matter-of-factly.

"Why don't they attack us while we are in this truck?" I asked.

He said somehow they knew we wouldn't bother them. But we could not leave the truck. They looked so adorable, and I wanted to climb down from the safety of that truck and pet them. Of course, that would have been my last conscious act on the face of the earth before I became a nice lunch entrée.

There is coming a day when Christ will reign and it no longer will be necessary to appreciate wild animals strictly from afar. We can take a walk with a lion or swim with a whale.

The animal kingdom will be subdued.

Also during the millennial reign of Christ will be universal justice and righteousness. No more corrupt lawyers and judges. No more frivolous lawsuits. No more corrupt rulings by judges with a liberal agenda. Psalm 72 says, "He will judge Your people with righteousness, and Your poor with justice. He will bring justice to the poor of the people; He will save the children of the needy, and will break in pieces the oppressor" (vv. 2-4).

During the millennial reign of Christ, the whole world will be a paradise. What a wonderful day that will be. While this is a day yet in the future, the Rapture, when the Lord comes for His Church, could happen at any moment. Christ is coming back. And all around us are signs of the times.

FROM TIME TO ETERNITY

CHAPTER 7

THEN I, JOHN, SAW THE HOLY CITY, NEW JERUSALEM,
COMING DOWN OUT OF HEAVEN FROM GOD, PREPARED AS
A BRIDE ADORNED FOR HER HUSBAND.

REVELATION 21:2

A father and son were driving along one afternoon when a bee flew into the car and started buzzing around. The little boy was terrified, because he was severely allergic to bees. One sting could actually kill him. His father told him, "Don't worry any longer, Son."

"But, Daddy, there is a bee in the car."

"Don't worry about the bee. I have taken care of it. Look." The father opened up his hand, and there was the bee, which had stung him. He said, "Son, I have taken the sting of the bee. It cannot hurt you now."

This is exactly what Jesus Christ did when He died on the cross for us. He took the sting of death. The apostle Paul writes in 1 Corinthians 15:55-57: "'O Death, where is your sting? . . .' The sting of death is sin, and the strength of sin is the law. But thanks be to God, who gives us the victory through our Lord Jesus Christ." Because of this, no Christian has to fear death.

Now, don't get me wrong. No one should love life more than a Christian. But Christians don't need to be terrified of death. Although we live in a world plagued by ongoing violence, wars, terrorism, disease and even natural disasters, we can confidently say, "If I die, I go to heaven. If I live, I serve the Lord. It is a win-win situation." This is the hope that every believer has.

THE TWO DEATHS

If you are an unbeliever, however, it is a different story altogether. The Bible teaches there are two deaths: a physical one and a spiritual one. Jesus warned that we are to fear the second death more than the first. Revelation 20:14 says, "Then Death and Hades were cast into the lake of fire. This is the second death." Revelation 21:8 states, "But the cowardly, unbelieving, abominable, murderers, sexually immoral, sorcerers, idolaters, and all liars shall have their part in the lake which burns with fire and brimstone, which is the second death."

The first death is physical death, but the second death is standing before God in the final judgment and being sent to hell for all eternity (see Heb. 9:27). If you are born once, you will die twice. But if you are born twice, you will die once. In other words, those who have not trusted in Jesus Christ need to know that a judgment is coming. But those who have put their faith in Jesus Christ will be spared from eternal punishment. As Romans 5:9 promises, "Since we have been made right in God's sight by the blood of Christ, he will certainly save us from God's judgment" (*NLT*).

THE TWO JUDGMENTS

The Bible does teach that Christians will be judged in what is called the Judgment Seat of Christ (see chapter 3). The Judgment Seat of Christ will take place in heaven and has to do with rewards. The Great White Throne Judgment, on the other hand, is what unbelievers will face. It is described in Revelation 20:

> And I saw a great white throne, and I saw the one who was sitting on it. The earth and sky fled from his presence, but they found no place to hide. I saw the dead, both great and small, standing before God's throne. And the books were

opened, including the Book of Life. And the dead were judged according to the things written in the books, according to what they had done (vv. 11-12, *NLT*).

Everyone who rejected God's offer of forgiveness through Christ will be present at the Great White Throne Judgment—the rich and famous, as well as the poor and unknown. No matter who they were on this earth, no matter how many albums they sold or how many movies they made or how many billions of dollars they were worth, everyone who did not put their faith in Jesus Christ will be there.

> **The big question at the Great White Throne of Judgment will be, "What have you done with Jesus Christ?" That is what God will want to know from you.**

Once a person reaches the Great White Throne Judgment, there is no turning back. It could be compared to being arrested, charged and put in jail for a crime of which you are guilty. After a period of time, you will make an appearance before the judge for sentencing. This is what this judgment will be like for unbelievers. There is no getting out of it. The sentence will be handed down.

On what basis will a person be judged? The issue at the Great White Throne of Judgment will not be how good you are, nor will it be how bad you are. It is not as much of a sin issue as it is a Son issue. The big question at this judgment will be, "What have you done with Jesus Christ?" That is what God will want to know from you.

We might wonder what the purpose of the Great White Throne of Judgment would be if unbelievers have already been condemned. Why even put them through this? The purpose of this judgment will be to clearly demonstrate, to anyone who would want to know, the reason why they are condemned.

This is important, because there is a lot of misunderstanding about who will go to heaven and who will go to hell. Whenever surveys have been taken in which people are asked if they believe in the afterlife, most people say they do. Most people think they will go to heaven. Interestingly, a lot of those same people think their friends will go to hell. A lot of people assume that they will go to heaven because they are good people and have lived a good life. But who defines what a good person is and what a good life is? These individuals do, of course. When asked who will go to hell, their answer will be along the lines of, "A bad person" or "Someone who lived a bad life." But these assumptions are simply not biblical.

The fact is, a person could live the worst life imaginable and then repent and come to faith in Jesus Christ on his or her deathbed. Amazingly, because of the grace of God, that person would go to heaven. Then again, a person could live a relatively good and moral life, but if he or she did not repent and trust in Christ, that person would go to hell. Jesus said in John 3:18, "He who believes in Him is not condemned; but he who does not believe is condemned already, because he has not believed in the name of the only begotten Son of God" (*NLT*). Those who are present at the Great White Throne of Judgment will be there because they did not believe.

Some may think this doesn't seem fair. But who are we to determine what is or is not fair? Throughout Scripture, we see that God is good. If God does something, it is good. But if God does not do something, then He has a reason for it. God is the One who determines what right and wrong are. He determines what is fair and what is not, not you or me.

In fact, if God were to act strictly on the basis of fairness, we would all be in trouble. One prayer I never offer up to God is "Give me everything I deserve," because in reality, I deserve judgment—and by the way, you do too. We all have broken God's commandments. We should be very thankful that God doesn't give us what we deserve. As Lamentations 3:22 says, "Through the Lord's mercies we are not consumed, because His compassions fail not. They are new every morning; Great is Your faithfulness." We had better be careful about raising fairness issues with God.

OPENED BOOKS

In the Bible's description of the Great White Throne of Judgment, we read that books will be opened: "And the books were opened, including the Book of Life. And the dead were judged according to the things written in the books, according to what they had done" (Rev. 20:12, *NLT*). What are these books, and what is written in them?

We are not told in Revelation, but by looking at other Scripture, we might conclude that one of these books would be the book of God's Law. Anyone who has been exposed to the truth of God's Law will be held accountable for what they know. According to Romans 3:19, "The law applies to those to whom it was given, for its purpose is to keep people from having excuses and to bring the entire world into judgment before God" (*NLT*). The reason people feel guilt is because they are guilty. God's law shows us that.

Someone might claim that they don't need Jesus Christ, because they live by the Ten Commandments (never mind the fact that most people cannot even name all of them). My question to that person would be, "Have you ever broken any of them? For instance, have you ever taken the Lord's name in vain?" By the way, taking the Lord's name in vain isn't limited to cursing. It is also using the Lord's name in a frivolous or insincere way. For example, there are a lot of people who will say they love Jesus and not mean it at all.

Have you ever lied? Have you ever stolen? Have you ever hated someone in your heart? Have you ever been guilty of sexual sin? Have you ever lusted after a man or woman? Have you ever coveted what someone else had? If you can say yes to any of these questions, then the Bible says that you are guilty of all of them: "For whoever shall keep the whole law, and yet stumble in one point, he is guilty of all" (Jas. 2:10). Who can live up to these standards? No one. The commandments were not given to make us righteous. They were given to show us that we need help. They were given to close our mouths and open our eyes. The Bible says, "Now we know that whatever the law says, it says to those who are under the law, so that every mouth may be silenced and the whole world held accountable to God" (Rom. 3:19, *NIV*).

So I believe one of these books mentioned in Revelation 20:12 would be the commandments of God, in order to clearly demonstrate that we have violated them. We have all broken God's commandments, not just once or twice, but many times (see Rom. 3:23). Being a "good person" won't be enough.

I believe another book at the Great White Throne of Judgment might be a record of everything that a person has said or done. According to Ecclesiastes 12:14, "God will judge us for everything we do, including every secret thing, whether good or bad" (*NLT*). Think about that—everything you have ever done is recorded. Also, every word that you have spoken is recorded, because Jesus said, "For every idle word men may speak, they will give account of it in the day of judgment. For by your words you will be justified, and by your words you will be condemned" (Matt. 12:36-37).

Still another book may be a record of how a person failed to live up to his or her own standards. There are a lot of people who say they don't believe in organized religion. They have their own beliefs. But we don't even live up to our own standards, much less God's. We don't live according to the codes that we establish for ourselves. Romans 2:14-16 says:

> Even when Gentiles, who do not have God's written
> law, instinctively follow what the law says, they show
> that in their hearts they know right from wrong. They
> demonstrate that God's law is written within them, for
> their own consciences either accuse them or tell them
> they are doing what is right. The day will surely come
> when God, by Jesus Christ, will judge everyone's secret
> life (*NLT*).

I think another book might be a record of every time a person has heard the gospel, so that he or she will not be able to
claim ignorance and say, "No one ever told me. I have never
heard that Jesus Christ was the only way to God. No one ever
told me that He died on a cross for me and that I needed to turn
from my sin and believe in Him." God keeps very accurate
records, and I am sure He has recorded all the times a person has
heard the gospel message and failed to respond.

Before we move on to the next book, the Book of Life, I want
to point out an important statement in Revelation 20:13-14:

> The sea gave up the dead who were in it, and Death and
> Hades delivered up the dead who were in them. And they
> were judged, each one according to his works. Then
> Death and Hades were cast into the lake of fire. This is
> the second death.

Notice the word "Hades" is used. When a nonbeliever dies,
he or she doesn't go immediately to the Great White Throne of
Judgment. This judgment will take place in the future, following
the millennial reign of Christ. It will occur at the same time for
every person.

So what happens to unbelievers when they die? Scripture teaches that they go to Hades. Notice verse 13 says, "Death and Hades delivered up the dead who were in them." In a sense, you could say that when unbelievers die, they go to a type of waiting area. Coming back to my earlier point, it would be a bit like waiting in jail before you are sent to prison. But this waiting area is a horrific place.

LAZARUS AND THE RICH MAN

In Luke 16, Jesus told a story that gives us a rare, behind-the-scenes look at what is happening in the invisible, supernatural world in this place called Hades. It is a story about a rich man and a beggar named Lazarus.

This rich man was living the dream life, while right outside of the gates of his estate was Lazarus, who was so impoverished that he lived off the bread the rich man wiped his hands with. They didn't have napkins in those days, so people would wipe their hands with pieces of bread. Then they would throw the bread on the ground, and the dogs would eat it. This was the type of food that sustained poor Lazarus.

One day, both men died. The rich man, who lived for pleasure, probably had a lavish funeral. But he went to a place of torment. Lazarus, who lived in abject poverty, probably had the most miserable existence imaginable. Yet he was taken to a place of comfort. Luke 16:22 says, "So it was that the beggar died, and was carried by the angels to Abraham's bosom."

Death is no respecter of persons. It is the great equalizer. Regardless of your position on Earth, it may be a different thing altogether on the other side. It is important to understand that the rich man's sin was not being wealthy. His sin was unbelief in God, indicated by his selfishness and self-obsession. But in contrast, Lazarus did believe.

This reminds us that when believers die, angels usher us into heaven. But prior to the death of a believer, the job of the angels is one of protection. Hebrews 1:14, speaking of angels, says, "Are they not all ministering spirits sent forth to minister for those who will inherit salvation?" The angels ministered to Lazarus, but this did not happen in the case of the rich man.

From Jesus' story, we note that Hades, at this point, was in two sections: one was a place of comfort, while the other was a place of torment. The rich man was able to make a request of Abraham, asking him to send Lazarus with a drop of water to cool his tongue.

When Jesus died on the cross, He went down to this place of comfort in Hades and took with Him to heaven all of the true believers who had died. Ever since that time, when believers die, they go to heaven, into the presence of God (see 2 Cor. 5:6-8). When unbelievers die, however, they go to the same place that this rich man went. Then, at the Great White Throne of Judgment, death and Hades deliver up the dead so that they can stand before God.

Jesus used the word "torment," or some form of it, four times in this story. This tells us that people in Hades are fully conscious, and they are in pain. They don't go into a state of suspended animation or some kind of soul sleep. They are not reincarnated to return to Earth as a higher or lower life form. Nor do they go to a place called purgatory. Once a person dies, he or she will go either to heaven or to hell, in this case, Hades, ultimately to stand before God at the Great White Throne of Judgment and then be cast into the lake of fire.

It is important for us to realize the story Jesus told in Luke 16 was a true story and not a parable. Jesus told many parables, which were illustrations (a parable has been defined as an earthly story with a heavenly meaning). In contrast to a parable, Jesus named specific people—Lazarus and a certain rich man. It was clear these were actual people. In a sense, Jesus was offering a glimpse behind the veil of eternity.

It is also clear that once you are on the other side, you cannot communicate with people here on Earth, and they cannot communicate with you. A story is told of the magician Harry Houdini, who insisted that a telephone be placed in his coffin when he died so that he could communicate from the other side. Let's just say that Harry never called.

THE BOOK OF LIFE

With this in mind, let's go back to Revelation 20. All of the books have been opened, and then the book that really matters—the Book of Life—is opened. Verse 15 says, "And anyone not found written in the Book of Life was cast into the lake of fire."

The nail-scarred hand of Jesus will begin to search this book for names. Not finding the name of the person standing before Him, Jesus will sadly but firmly say, "Depart from Me, you cursed, into the everlasting fire prepared for the devil and his angels" (Matt. 25:41). Some will protest and say, "Lord, Lord, did we not prophesy in your name? Did we not do many wonderful works in your name? Did we not cast out demons in your name?" Others might say, "Did we not go to church twice a year in your name? Were we not baptized in your name? Did we not receive communion in your name?" But Jesus will say, "Depart from Me."

If we put our faith in Jesus Christ and turn from our sin, our names will be found in the Book of Life and we will be welcomed into heaven.

There will be people on that final day who might boast of their religious activity, but they never put their faith in Jesus and accepted God's offer of forgiveness. Every one of us has sinned. Every one of us deserves to go to hell. But if we put our faith in

Jesus Christ and turn from our sin, our names will be found in the Book of Life and we will be welcomed into heaven. If we reject God's offer of forgiveness, then we will face this certain judgment.

Hell was prepared for the devil and his angels. God did not create hell for people. It is God's desire that every man and woman created in His image join Him in that wonderful place called heaven. But if we reject His offer of forgiveness through His Son, then on that final day, we will have no one to blame but ourselves.

GOD'S FREE GIFT

Many people take God's gift of eternal life for granted. Just think about it. God Almighty says, "I have the most wonderful present for you. It is the gift of eternal life."

"How much will it cost?" they ask.

"You couldn't afford it," God says. "It already has been paid for. Receive it." Yet all too often, the gift God so freely offers lays unclaimed.

A number of years ago, I was given some free tickets to Disneyland. Someone was going to meet us there but wasn't able to come. As we walked into the park, I had the extra ticket in my pocket, which would admit anyone. I started feeling guilty, so I said to my wife, "I'm going to give this ticket to someone. This will be the easiest thing I ever did. See you in two minutes." However, when I went out and tried to give away the ticket, the people I approached would cautiously back away.

"What's wrong?" I would ask. "It is a free ticket to Disneyland."

"Why are you offering it to me?"

"The person who was supposed to use it wasn't able to come. I want to give it to someone." When all was said and done, it took me 25 minutes to give away that ticket! Everyone was suspicious, because no one gives away free tickets to Disneyland.

In the same way, when God offers the gift of eternal life, people are often suspicious. "What's the catch?" they want to know. While this gift God offers is free, it doesn't mean that it is cheap. It cost Him everything. That is why it is an insult to God to turn His gift down. He has offered the greatest thing He can offer: the death of His own dear Son. Yet many people have the audacity to say, "Not now" or "Later" or "I am too busy."

C. S. Lewis once said that no one ever goes to heaven deservingly, and no one ever goes to hell unwillingly. Tragically, there will be people who will turn down God's priceless gift and will find themselves in this place of judgment. On that final day, they will have no one to blame but themselves.

WHEN FOREVER BEGINS

On the other hand, there is a glorious future awaiting those who have accepted God's gift of eternal life. We have heard the expression, "It is like heaven on earth." In Revelation 21, we find a literal fulfillment of that statement. Heaven and earth come together.

> Now I saw a new heaven and a new earth, for the first heaven and the first earth had passed away. Also there was no more sea. Then I, John, saw the holy city, New Jerusalem, coming down out of heaven from God, prepared as a bride adorned for her husband. And I heard a loud voice from heaven saying, "Behold, the tabernacle of God is with men, and He will dwell with them, and they shall be His people. God Himself will be with them and be their God. And God will wipe away every tear from their eyes; there shall be no more death, nor sorrow, nor crying. There shall be no more pain, for the former things have passed away." Then He who sat on the throne said, "Behold, I make all things new" (vv. 1-5).

At this point, we will have passed from the realm of time into the realm of eternity. Heaven and earth will have merged and become one. These verses call to mind the classic hymn "Amazing Grace": "When we've been there ten thousand years, bright shining as the sun, we've no less days to sing God's praise than when we'd first begun."[1] What an apt description of what is ahead for every true believer.

Note

1. John Newton, "Amazing Grace," *Olney Hymns* (London: W. Oliver, 1779). This final stanza, by an unknown author, first appeared in the *Baptist Songster* by R. Winchell in 1829. http://www.cyberhymnal.org/htm/a/m/amazgrac.htm (accessed September 2005).

WHILE YOU WAIT

During the course of his travels, a dignitary arrived in a small town, where he paid a visit to a one-room school. Of course, all of the students were greatly impressed that a person of such importance would come to visit them. As he was preparing to leave, the dignitary told the students that he would come again, but he did not tell them when that would be. When he returned, he added, he would bring a prize to the student with the cleanest desk.

The dignitary left, and one little girl, who was known for her messiness, announced that she was going to win the prize. The other students laughed, because she always had a cluttered desk. There was always trash all over it, and it was disorganized on the inside. Everyone laughed at the idea that she would be ready when the dignitary returned. So she told them, "From now on, I will clean my desk every Monday morning."

They said, "Suppose he comes on Friday?"

"Well, then, I will clean it every morning," she said.

Someone said, "But what if he comes at the end of the day?" She was quiet for a moment, then her face lit up.

"I know what I will do!" she said. "I will keep my desk clean all of the time."

Now, that little girl has the right idea. Clearly, we know that the Lord is coming back again. In the New Testament's 260 chapters, the return of Jesus Christ is mentioned no fewer than 318 times. The New Testament speaks constantly about the Lord's return.

CHAPTER 8

In the previous chapters of this book, I have pointed to the fact that all around us are signs of the times—reminders that Jesus Christ could come back at any moment. We have caught a glimpse of the prophetic picture that has been painted for us in Scripture. I have stated that it is my belief that the next event on the prophetic calendar will most likely be the Rapture of the Church, when "the Lord Himself will descend from heaven with a shout, with the voice of an archangel, and with the trumpet of God" (1 Thess. 4:16), and we will be caught up to meet the Lord in the air.

I have also stated that sometime either before, during or after the Rapture, we will see a large force from the extreme north of Israel, identified as Magog (considered by many to be modern-day Russia), come and invade her. The Tribulation period will begin, inaugurated by the emergence of the Antichrist, and will last for seven years. The last three and a half years will be a literal hell on Earth. The world will then experience war on a scale such as humanity has never seen, culminating in the battle to end all battles, the Battle of Armageddon, which will be fought in the Middle East in a valley called Megiddo.

Jesus Christ will then return to the earth in the Second Coming, and He will rule and reign for 1,000 years. During this time, Satan will have been chained up, but he will be released for a short time after the 1,000 years are finished. Then Satan will be cast into the lake of fire. Also at this time, the Great White Throne of Judgment will take place, where every man and woman who has not put his or her faith in Christ will stand before God and will know why he or she is facing this judgment. These people, too, will be cast into the lake of fire, because their names will not be found in the Book of Life. But those who have put their faith in Christ—those whose names are written in the Book of Life—will enter into eternity in God's presence.

READY FOR THE RAPTURE

In light of all these things, how should we be living right now? What are we supposed to be doing while we wait for Christ's return? Along with a number of other verses in Scripture, 1 John 2:28 provides the answer to that question: "And now, dear children, continue to live in fellowship with Christ so that when he returns, you will be full of courage and not shrink back from him in shame" (*NLT*).

This verse reveals two very important attitudes concerning our reaction to the Lord's return: either we will be full of courage or we will shrink back from Him in shame. The difference depends on the condition of those who are waiting. If you are in fellowship with Jesus right now, then you will be full of courage. When you see all the reminders that Christ is coming back, you will think, *I am ready.* But if you are not walking with God, you will dread Christ's return and shrink back in shame.

Your response to the very mention of the Lord's imminent return is, in many ways, a spiritual barometer of your relationship with Christ. If your life is where it ought to be, then you will be passionate and excited about the Lord's return. You **If you are in fellowship with Jesus, you will be full of courage. But if you are not walking with God, you will dread Christ's return and shrink back in shame.** will eagerly anticipate it. But if your relationship with Christ is not what it should be, then you will be frightened, alarmed and ashamed at the idea of His returning, because you will be afraid that you might be caught doing something you know you shouldn't be doing. A messy desk will be the least of your problems.

Take the workplace, for example. Let's say some employees are goofing off, when all of a sudden, someone whispers, "The boss is coming." Immediately, the employees change their behavior. They stop what they are doing and start looking busy. Why? They know the boss signs their paychecks, and they would like to keep getting them. On the other hand, if an employee is working hard and someone says, "The boss is coming," then that employee doesn't need to do anything differently. Why? Because that employee is already doing what he or she is supposed to be doing. There is nothing to be ashamed of if the boss shows up unexpectedly.

If you are a true Christian, your attitude should be such that whether the Lord comes today, tomorrow, a year from now or 10 years from now, it doesn't matter. You are ready and looking forward to it.

IS GOD RUNNING LATE?

As we look at this world in which we live, especially since 9/11, we wonder how much worse things will get. Every time we open the newspaper, turn on the radio or TV, or surf the Internet, it seems as though there is more bad news. Another frightening possibility or scenario begins to unfold. We wonder, *Is the Lord late? Has God forgotten about us?*

Absolutely not. God is precisely on schedule. As 2 Peter 3 tells us:

The Lord isn't really being slow about his promise to return, as some people think. No, he is being patient for your sake. He does not want anyone to perish, so he is giving more time for everyone to repent. And so, dear friends, while you are waiting for these things to happen, make every effort to live a pure and blameless life. And be at peace with God (vv. 9,14, *NLT*).

When I was in school, I was frequently tardy. So, many times a teacher would say to me, "Greg, you are tardy again. Go to the vice principal's office." But the Lord is not tardy. He is not late.

He is exactly on time. He hasn't come back yet because He is waiting for more people to come into His kingdom.

I became a Christian in 1970, when I was a teenager. I was hoping Jesus would come back any day. In fact, my Christian friends and I prayed for the Lord to return. I am sure there are a few people reading this today who are glad that He didn't answer our prayers, because they have come to faith in Christ since that time. I believe the Lord is waiting for one last person to believe, and then the Rapture can take place and we will be out of here.

EYES ON THE SKY

In the meantime, we need to be in a constant state of readiness. In Luke 12, Jesus illustrated this fact with a parable about an expectant servant:

> Let your waist be girded and your lamps burning; and you yourselves be like men who wait for their master, when he will return from the wedding, that when he comes and knocks they may open to him immediately. Blessed are those servants whom the master, when he comes, will find watching. Assuredly, I say to you that he will gird himself and have them sit down to eat, and will come and serve them. And if he should come in the second watch, or come in the third watch, and find them so, blessed are those servants. But know this, that if the master of the house had known what hour the thief would come, he would have watched and not allowed his house to be broken into. Therefore you also be ready, for the Son of Man is coming at an hour you do not expect (vv. 35-40).

In verse 35, Jesus turned to an example that would have been readily understood by everyone in this culture: a servant waiting for his master to return from a wedding. Weddings in our culture today are usually planned well in advance. They take place at a specific location, which has been specified by the bride and groom on a wedding invitation that has been mailed to their guests a number of weeks earlier. The ceremony and reception are completed in a matter of hours.

But in Jesus' day, a wedding would last up to a week. It was a joyous, festive gathering of family and friends, much like our weddings today. But often, the time of the groom's arrival remained a mystery. So the announcement could be made to the guests in the middle of the afternoon or in the middle of the night, "The bridegroom is coming!" Those who weren't ready to go at a moment's notice would miss the wedding. So when Jesus said, "Let your waist be girded and your lamps burning," he was saying, "Be ready."

Back in those days, everyone wore long, flowing robes. To move quickly, people would pull their robes above their knees and cinch in their belt. Having your waist "girded" meant having your robes pulled up and your belt tightened to ensure freedom of movement.

As well as having your waist girded, Jesus mentioned having "your lamps burning." Back then, a portable source of light consisted of a clay saucer that held oil and a wick. Light the wick, and the oil lamp would light the way. It was like a first-century flashlight. Had Jesus been speaking to a twenty-first century audience, perhaps He may have said, "Be ready to go and have fresh batteries in your flashlight so you will know where you're going."

Jesus was saying that in light of the fact that He could come back at any time, we need to be alert, mobile and prepared. We need to be in a constant state of readiness, even if He does not come as quickly as we would like Him to.

Jesus continued, "And if he should come in the second watch, or come in the third watch, and find them so, blessed are those servants" (v. 38). Back then, the night hours were divided into four watches. The first watch was from 6:00 to 9:00 P.M., the second watch was from 9:00 P.M. to 12:00 A.M., the third watch was from 12:00 A.M to 3:00 A.M., and the fourth watch consisted of the time just before dawn. Jesus was saying, "Even if I come later than you originally expected, be ready."

One night, Jesus sent His disciples to the other side of the Sea of Galilee, while He stayed behind to pray. As the disciples were making their way across the Sea of Galilee, a great storm arose, which became so powerful that they thought they were going to die. What they didn't real ize was that Jesus never lost sight of them. They may have lost sight of Jesus because of the storm, but He never lost sight of them.

We need to be alert, mobile and prepared. We need to be in a constant state of readiness, even if Christ does not come as quickly as we would like Him to.

Then the Bible says, "Now in the fourth watch of the night Jesus went to them, walking on the sea" (Matt. 14:25). Jesus left them in that stormy situation for most of the night. They had been fighting the storm for nine hours at that point. Just when it seemed all was lost and they wouldn't make it, Jesus himself came strolling across water. Everything changed with His arrival. Maybe Jesus wanted them to completely exhaust their resources so that they would realize their only way out was through Him.

Like the disciples, we are all going through storms in life. At times, it seems as though we can't take anymore. The Lord may come a little later than we expect, but He will come. Maybe the Lord is waiting for us to come to the same point the disciples did. Maybe He is waiting for us to realize that the problems we are facing are greater than an economic, military or political solution can resolve. Maybe He is waiting for us to see that we can't fix this with intelligence or technology alone. Maybe God is waiting for us to ask for His help and to return to Him once more.

FOUR THINGS WE SHOULD DO

In the meantime, what should we, as Christians, be doing?

1. Be Watching for Him

First, we need to be watching for Him. Jesus said, "Blessed are those servants whom the master, when he comes, will find watching" (Luke 12:37). As Christians, we need to be paying careful attention to this world around us, and at the same time, keep the lightest hold possible on the things of this world.

Obviously, we have to live in this world, but this doesn't that mean we have to love this world. In other words, we should be careful that we don't become so involved in the things of this life that we forget about what really matters. Colossians 3:1-2 tells us, "Since you have been raised to new life with Christ, set your sights on the realities of heaven, where Christ sits at God's right hand in the place of honor and power. Let heaven fill your thoughts. Do not think only about things down here on earth" (*NLT*). Be heavenly minded. I'm aware of the old adage that says, "He is so heavenly minded that he is no earthly good." But that is not a correct statement. If you are truly heavenly minded, then you will be of great earthly good.

Jesus said, "Don't worry about having enough food or drink or clothing. Why be like the pagans who are so deeply concerned about these things? Your heavenly Father already knows all your needs, and he will give you all you need from day to day if you live for him and make the Kingdom of God your primary concern" (Matt. 6:31-33, *NLT*). We need to be watching for His return.

2. Be Ready to Go

When I leave on a trip, I always pack my bags the night before. That way, I'm ready to go when it's time to leave. That is the idea of what Jesus was saying. Be ready to go on a moment's notice.

If the Lord said today is the day, your bags should be packed and your affairs should be in order.

We should not be doing anything that we would be ashamed to be doing when Jesus comes back again. You should be ready for His return. First John 3:2 says, "Beloved, now we are children of God; and it has not yet been revealed what we shall be, but we know that when He is revealed, we shall be like Him, for we shall see Him as He is." We should be living in such a way that we want to get closer to the Lord each and every day. This was the attitude of the apostle Paul, who said:

> I don't mean to say that I have already achieved these things or that I have already reached perfection! But I keep working toward that day when I will finally be all that Christ Jesus saved me for and wants me to be. No, dear friends, I am still not all I should be, but I am focusing all my energies on this one thing: Forgetting the past and looking forward to what lies ahead, I strain to reach the end of the race and receive the prize for which God, through Christ Jesus, is calling us up to heaven (Phil. 3:12-14, *NLT*).

Is your life right with God right now? Are there some things that you should change?

3. Be Anxiously Awaiting His Return

We should not only be ready, but we should also be anxiously awaiting Christ's return. Jesus said, "And you yourselves be like men who wait for their master, when he will return from the wedding, that when he comes and knocks they may open to him immediately" (Luke 12:36).

My dog likes to sleep against the door of my bedroom. I know this because when he scratches during the night, it sounds like someone is knocking at the door. Sometimes, when I get up in the morning and open the door, he rolls in. He has one thing on his mind: a walk. Everywhere I go, he is there waiting, nudging up against me. Every morning, he leans up against the door, anxiously awaiting my arrival.

Have you ever invited someone over to your house and were so anxious for them to get there that you opened the door before they knocked? That is how we need to be in these last days. We need to be anxiously awaiting the Lord's return.

4. Be Working

Finally, we should be working. Luke 12:43 says, "Blessed is that servant whom his master will find so doing when he comes." If watching is the evidence of faith, then working is the evidence of faith in action. Watching for the Lord's return will help us prepare our lives, but working will assure that we bring others with us. Notice that Jesus used the word "blessed" in connection with living this way. "Blessed" means "happy." It is a happy thing to be a Christian. It is a happy thing to look for the Lord's return. It is a happy thing to have your sin forgiven. There is joy in this.

Don't get the wrong impression and think that Christians can't have any fun because we are waiting for the Lord's return. We should live our lives to the fullest. We should enjoy and savor each moment as a gift from God. We don't need artificial stimulants like drugs and alcohol to cope. We don't need all these things the world tells us we need to make us happy, because we have this relationship with God through Jesus Christ. In light of the fact that the Lord is coming back again, we ought to be living pure and blameless lives. Blessed is the person who lives this way. If you want to live a happy life, then live in such a way that you are constantly ready for the Lord's return.

Jesus is coming back. It could be at midnight. It could be at noon. It could be today or a year from now. No one knows for sure when He is coming. So keep your desk clean all the time. Keep your life right with Him.

HOW TO BE READY

Perhaps as you have read this book, you have become aware of the fact that you are not ready for the Lord's return. You are afraid that you will be one of those who will be left behind when Jesus calls His Church home to heaven.

It doesn't have to be that way. You can commit your life to Jesus Christ right now and have the assurance that you will indeed be ready for His return and will be one of those who will get to heaven for sure. Whether it be by Rapture or death, your future heavenly home will be awaiting you.

Jesus Christ is coming. Are you ready to meet Him? If He were to come back tonight, are you certain that you would go to heaven? If you aren't certain, then you can be. Here's what you need to do:

1. *Realize that you are a sinner who needs a Savior.* The Bible teaches that all of us have sinned and fallen short of God's glory (see Rom. 3:23). No matter how good a life we try to live, we still fall miserably short of being a good person. We have all failed to live up to God's holy standards, and we have all crossed the line repeatedly. It's easy to blame others for our sinful behavior, but the fact is that we are personally respon-sible for the sins that we have committed. The Bible says, "No one is good—not even one" (Rom. 3:10, *NLT*). We cannot become who we are supposed to be without Jesus Christ.

2. *Recognize that Jesus Christ died on the cross for your sins.* Because you have broken God's commandments and there was no way for you to atone for your own sins,

God took radical measures and sent His own Son, Jesus Christ, to die on the cross in your place and pay the price for your sin. The Bible tells us, "But God showed His great love for us by sending Christ to die for us while were still sinners" (Rom. 5:8, *NLT*). This is the good news, that God loves us so much that He sent His only Son to die in our place when we least deserved it.

3. *Repent of your sin.* The Bible tells us to "repent therefore and be converted" (Acts 3:19). The word "repent" means to be sorry for and to change one's direction in life. It is to turn to God and away from known sin. Instead of running away from God, we can run toward Him.

4. *Receive Jesus Christ into your life.* Becoming a Christian is not merely believing some creed or going to church on Sunday. To be a Christian is to have Christ Himself come and live in your heart as Savior and Lord. The Bible says, "But as many as received Him, to them He gave the right to become children of God, to those who believe in His name" (John 1:12). You must receive Christ into your life. Jesus Himself said, "Behold, I stand at the door and knock. If anyone hears My voice and opens the door, I will come in to him and dine with him, and he with Me" (Rev. 3:20).

The way you receive Christ into your life is through prayer. You can even pray this prayer right now and Jesus will come and take residence in your heart and give you the assurance that you will indeed be ready for His return.

Lord Jesus, I know that I am a sinner. I have broken Your commandments and sinned against You. But You loved me so

much that You died on the cross in my place. Lord, come and take residence in my heart. Forgive me of my sins. I turn from those things that would displease You right now. Fill me with Your Holy Spirit and help me to follow You all the days of my life. Thank You for hearing and answering this prayer.
In Jesus' name I pray, amen.

The Bible tells us, "If we confess our sins, he is faithful and just to forgive us our sins and cleanse us from all unrighteousness" (1 John 1:9). If you just prayed that prayer and meant it, then I want you to know, on the authority of God's Word, that Jesus Christ has come to live in your heart! Your decision to follow Christ means that God has forgiven you and that you will spend eternity in heaven. It means you will be ready to meet Christ when He returns.

To help you grow in your newfound faith, be sure to spend time regularly reading the Bible, praying, spending time with other Christians by going to church, and telling others about your faith in Christ. For additional resources to help you learn more about what it means to be a follower of Jesus Christ, please write or e-mail me at the following address and I will send you some follow-up materials that will help you grow spiritually.

Greg Laurie
Harvest Ministries
6115 Arlington Avenue
Riverside, CA 92504
Greg@Harvest.org
http://www.harvest.org/knowgod

A PRAYER FOR LAST DAYS BELIEVERS

Father, we believe that we are living in the last days.
We believe that Jesus is coming back to this earth to establish
His kingdom. We see what the enemy is doing around us today.
We see some who have thrown in the towel and have abandoned
their faith, and we see that temptation is strong in these days.

It is our prayer, Lord, that not one of us will become a casualty,
that not one of us will fall away from You. Instead, may we recommit
ourselves with greater intensity than ever before. May we finish
this race we are running with joy.

So Lord, let Your Word sink deeply into our hearts.
May we be strengthened. May we become bolder. May we become
more committed as we learn what it is to live as believers
in these critical days.

This we would ask in Jesus' name, amen.

ABOUT THE AUTHOR

Greg Laurie, senior pastor of Harvest Christian Fellowship in Riverside, California, began his pastoral ministry at age 19 by leading a Bible study of 30 people, which God has since transformed into a congregation that is among the eight largest churches in America. In 1990, Greg began holding public evangelistic events called Harvest Crusades. Since then, nearly three million people have attended Harvest Crusades across the United States and in Australia. Greg is the featured speaker on the nationally syndicated radio program *A New Beginning,* heard nationwide and overseas. He is also the featured host of the television program *Harvest: Greg Laurie,* which is seen internationally. He is the author of a number of books, including the Gold Medallion Award-winner *The Upside-Down Church.* In addition, Greg has authored the study notes for two *New Living Translation* study Bibles. He and his wife, Cathe, have two children and live in Southern California.